THE NATIONAL
EDUCATION ASSOCIATION

A SPECIAL MISSION

Susan Lowell Butler

ACKNOWLEDGEMENTS

NEA: A Special Mission is a narrative of those events we believe to be the most important and significant in the Association's 129-year history. For those seeking more detail on the history of public education and NEA's role in it, see Dr. Edgar B. Wesley's centennial publication, *NEA: The First Hundred Years*. Other useful references include Dr. Allan West's *The National Education Association: The Power Base for Education* and Dr. Marshall Donley's 1975 work, *Power To The Teacher*. All of these works have been of assistance to me and I acknowledge my debt to their authors.

Susan Lowell Butler

Susan Lowell Butler worked for the NEA from 1970 to 1984 as an organizer, Director of Communications and Western States Regional Director. She lives and works in Austin, Texas.

Designed by William J. Kircher and Associates

Library of Congress Catalog Card Number 87–14195

ISBN 0-8106-1452-9

Published in 1987 by the National Education Association of the United States, 1201 16th Street, N.W., Washington, D.C. 20036

CONTENTS

IN THE BEGINNING
1857-1861

*I*t had been tried before—in 1830, and then twice in 1831, and again, as recently as 1849, when Horace Mann, the most reknowned educational leader of his time, founded the American Association for the Advancement of Education.

On four separate occasions efforts had been made by leading educational minds to create a national organization of teachers. All four efforts withered; none succeeded in capturing the loyalty and commitment of American educators.

Then, in 1857, as a troubled nation faced almost certain civil war, one effort, made by several determined men—"practical teachers" who had been founders and leaders of their state-level Associations—one effort finally took root and survived difficult years to grow and flourish throughout the United States.

The story of the National Education Association begins on a warm August day in 1857.

Without question, the issue of slavery dominated the minds and conversations of most Americans. The United States Supreme Court, in the *Dred Scott* decision, had essentially ruled that slaves were property. A proslavery constitution had been written for Kansas. The ruling class in the South—a "gentry" of no more than 15,000 families whose iron grip on the Southern economy thoroughly dominated economic and social decisions—clung fast to the notion that the South could not survive without continuation of "the peculiar institution" of slave-based agriculture. In 1857, a "prime field hand" sold for about $1,800. By 1860, the annual cotton crop would exceed 2.3 billion pounds per year, and reflect two-thirds of the exports of the United States. In the North, and elsewhere, the abolitionists were no less committed to an end to slavery; *Uncle Tom's Cabin* fueled feelings; and the conflicting views grew increasingly passionate and unyielding. The fight was for nothing less than the soul of a nation whose founding fathers had written in the Declaration of Independence, "We hold these Truths to be self-evident, that all Men are created equal. . ."

In 1857, James Buchanan had begun his Presidency of a nation that, with the exception of the growing preoccupation with slavery, was generally vigorous. Immigrants continued to seek the new nation's promise: more than 2,800,000 had come in 1846 alone, mainly from Ireland, Germany and England.

Philosophically, America was a nation wedded to the idea that continuing growth and prosperity was the natural condition of man. Fueled by philosophers like John Stuart Mill, American thinkers spread the concept that unregulated competition of ideas would yield truth, and that man was a perfectable creature, each individual capable of greatness and self-realization. The American expression of these beliefs flowered in the products of New England Transcendentalism, as delineated by Emerson's writings and in Thoreau's *Walden*, published in 1854. In New York, intellectuals debated such ideas in the new literary journals, *The Atlantic Monthly* and *Harper's*. Poet Walt Whitman in *Leaves of Grass*, first issued in 1855, captured the optimism and zest of mid-century America in which each person's energy and hard work could yield rewards of the pocketbook and of the spirit.

American opinions on education had reached consensus on several basic ideas: that there should be

free primary and secondary education for all children; that teachers should be professionally trained for their work; and that all children should be required to attend school until a certain age.

The negative element was the quality of that education. Most American teachers in 1857 worked in one-room schoolhouses, afflicted with salaries less than $100 per year, sparse teaching materials, and uncertain public support. Tenure was, of course, unheard of—and most teachers "kept school" only four or five months a year, forcing them to earn the rest of their living in farming or industry. Male teachers were paid as much as two-thirds more than women, and opportunities for advanced education and training were rare. Most educators had received meager educations, usually at "normal schools," and found their best opportunities to learn more and relieve their personal isolation by attending "institutes"—multiday training and lectures provided by traveling school superintendents and other administrators who journeyed around their jurisdictions on a periodic basis.

The other vehicle for learning and sharing was provided by meetings of state education Associations. These were usually a day or two in duration, and consisted largely of formal speeches and lectures on a wide variety of subjects. The Association meetings also served as a means for teachers to express themselves on education's problems and needs—and they did so by passing resolutions calling for equal pay for equal work, a voice in choosing texts and planning the curriculum, an end to school on Saturdays, and fair evaluations of performance.

State education Associations existed in fifteen states of the thirty-one in the Union: Rhode Island, New York, Massachusetts, Ohio, Connecticut, Vermont, Michigan, Pennsylvania, Wisconsin, Illinois, New Jersey, Iowa, New Hampshire, Indiana and Missouri. These were not yet organizations dedicated to the advancement of member rights—but they were the only existing vehicles for semiorganized teacher-to-teacher communication. As yet, there was no national organization to serve as a single clear voice for America's teachers and the growing public schools of the new nation.

The true "melting pot" of American culture was the school. Teachers were expected to integrate the large number of foreign-speaking students into the mainstream of American society, a task which the rest of society seemed willing to ignore. In 1909, a survey of major cities showed that more than half the students in any given classroom could not speak English.

Zalmon Richards, first president of the National Teachers Association, which became the National Education Association.

The Union Academy, the school of NTA's first president, Zalmon Richards.

''Believing that what has been accomplished for the states by state associations may be done for the whole country by a National Association, we, the undersigned, invite our fellow-educators throughout the United States to assemble . . . for the purpose of organizing a National Teachers Association . . . . We cordially extend this invitation to all practical teachers in the North, the South, the East, and the West, who are willing to unite in a general effort to promote the general welfare of our country by concentrating the wisdom and power of numerous minds, and distributing among all the accumulated experiences of all; who are ready to devote their energies and their means to advance the dignity, respectability and usefulness of their calling; and who, in fine, believe that the time has come when the teachers of the nation should gather into one great educational brotherhood. . . .''

August 26, 1857

From ''The Call,'' an invitation sent to teachers throughout the nation by the presidents of 10 state teachers' associations.

Thomas W. Valentine had written "The Call," an invitation sent out to teachers throughout the nation over the signatures of the presidents of ten state teachers' Associations—New York, Massachusetts, New Hampshire, Vermont, Pennsylvania, Indiana, Illinois, Wisconsin, Iowa, and Missouri.

Valentine was president of the New York State Teachers Association, and a grammar-school teacher in Brooklyn, New York. His close associate and fellow-organizer of the dream was Daniel B. Hagar, President of the Massachusetts Teachers Association and, at the time of the call, principal of the Salem Normal School.

One hundred educators answered the call, coming from eight states and the District of Columbia. In the ranks of the founders was Robert Campbell, a black man from Jamaica who had come to Philadelphia to teach at the Philadelphia Institute for Colored Children, and two women, Mrs. H.D. Conrad and Miss A.W. Beecher, from Dayton, Ohio.

The meeting's organizers had prepared a constitution for the Association, and the Preamble's stately simplicity (written by Hagar) expressed the mission in clear terms for all to understand: "To elevate the character and advance the interests of the profession of teaching, and to promote the cause of popular education in the United States. . ."

The Constitution was promptly adopted, and forty-three founders signed the document. Membership was restricted to "gentlemen," but the two women attending were permitted to sign, and the decision was made that women could be elected "honorary members" and present their views to the organization in the form of written essays to be read by a male member. This restriction, typical of the times, would not long endure in the National Teachers Association.

Zalmon Richards was elected to serve as the first president of NTA. Richards was the owner of his own school in Washington, D.C., the Union Academy. He had taught in village academies and country schools, conducted teachers' institutes, and had been principal of two academies before opening his own institution. He was destined to remain an active educator all his life, and an active participant in the affairs of the Association until his death in 1900.

Dues were set at $1.00 per year, and a life membership could be purchased for $10.00.

"Practical teachers," not the great educational solons of the time such as Horace Mann or Henry Barnard, had finally created a national organization that would grow and thrive and serve the teachers of the United States.

CONVENTIONS HELP SHAPE PUBLIC EDUCATION 1862-1899

SUPPLEMENT TO THE SCHOOL BULLETIN FOR MAY, 1892.

OFFICIAL BULLETIN

—— OF THE ——

National Educational Association.

Thirty-Second Annual Meeting, at Saratoga Springs, July 12 to 15, 1892.

C. W. BARDEEN, PUBLISHER, SYRACUSE, N. Y.

SECRETARY:
R. W. STEVENSON,
Sup't of Schools, Wichita, Ks.

PRESIDENT:
E. H. COOK,
Sup't of Schools, Flushing, N. Y.

FIRST VICE-PRESIDENT:
W. R. GARRETT,
State Sup't, Tennessee.

TREASURER:
J. M. GREENWOOD,
Sup't of Schools, Kansas City, Mo.

CHAIRMAN BOARD TRUSTEES:
NORMAN A. CALKINS,
Ass't Sup't, New York City.

A BRIEF HISTORY.

The National Educational Association was organized at Philadelphia, in 1857, under the name of the National Teachers' Association, by leading teachers from various sections of the country. James L. Enos was chairman of the first meeting, William E. Sheldon its first secretary, and A. J. Rickoff, its first treasurer. The name was changed in 1870 to National Educational Association.

The Association has held thirty-one meetings, as follows: Two at Philadelphia, 1857, 1879; one at Cincinnati, 1858; Washington, 1859; Buffalo, 1860; Chicago, 1863,1887; Ogdensburg, 1864; Harrisburg, 1865, Indianapolis, 1866; Nashville, 1868; 1880; Trenton, 1869; Cleveland, 1870; St. Louis, 1871; Boston, 1872; Elmira, 1873; Detroit, 1874; Minneapolis, 1875; Baltimore, 1876; Louisville, 1877; Chautauqua, 1880; Atlanta, 1881; three at Saratoga, 1882, 1883, 1885; Madison, 1884; Topeka, 1886; San Francisco, 1888; St. Paul, 1890; Toronto, 1891. There were no meetings in 1861, 1862, 1867, 1878.

Its presidents have been Zalmon Richards, A. J. Rickoff, J. W. Bulkley, John D. Philbrick, W. H. Wells, S. S. Greene, J. P. Wickersham, J. M. Gregory, L. Van Bokkelen, Daniel B. Hagar, J. L. Pickard, E. E. White, B. G. Northrop, S. H. White, Wm. T. Harris, Wm. F. Phelps, M. A. Newell, John Hancock, J. Ormond Wilson, James H. Smart, G. J. Orr, E. T. Tappan, Thomas W. Bicknell, N. A. Calkins, W. E. Sheldon, Aaron Gove, A. P. Marble, James H Canfield, and W. R. Garrett. It was incorporated Feb. 24, 1886, and has a permanent fund of nearly $50,000.

ITS OBJECTS.

"To elevate the character and advance the interests of the profession of teaching, and to promote the cause of popular education in the United States."

MEMBERSHIP.

Any person in any way connected with the work of education, or any Educational Association, shall be eligible to membership. Any such person may become a member of this Association by paying *two dollars* and signing the Constitution, and may continue a member by the payment of an annual fee of *two dollars*. On neglect to pay such fee, the membership will cease.

LIFE MEMBERSHIP.—Any person eligible to membership may become a *life member* by the payment, at one time, of *twenty dollars*.

LIFE DIRECTOR.— Any friend of education may become a life director by the donation of *one hundred dollars* to the Association, at one time, either by himself or on his behalf, and any Educational Association may secure a perpetual directorship by a like donation of *one hundred dollars*, the director to be appointed annually, or for life.

In 1892, NEA created the "Council of Ten" to recommend a program of instruction for the rapidly expanding high school system. Before, high school was seen as a luxury that most parents could ill afford. (Bulletin published for 1892.)

For the first thirty-five years of life, the Association's major activity was its regular conventions. These meetings, held nearly every year, served the educators and the burgeoning public schools of the nation as a forum in which all the ideas about schooling of the time were hotly debated and, in most cases, consensus achieved as to what course of action and study would best benefit American public education.

The American public schools in 1857 were unregulated by any actions of the federal government and, in that respect, very different from education systems elsewhere in the world which were largely shaped by the dictates of central governments.

American public education in these early days was chaotic, and the nation was distracted from attention to its schools by the trauma of the Civil War and other events. Had there not been an NTA—subsequently NEA—in these difficult years, and had its leaders not labored to bring some measure of standardization to schooling in local communities and states, progress toward uniform educational opportunity would have been greatly retarded. The Association in these days saw itself as charged with developing national policy on education; the work of improving the lot of "practical teachers" fell to the growing state Associations.

1862

Congress passed the *Morrill Act* (the Land Grant Act), which made possible the sale of public land to benefit agricultural education and paved the way for the creation of state universities. NTA supported the passage of this important early federal legislation on behalf of public education.

1863

NTA's fifth convention boasted 1,600 attendees and the passage of a resolution stating "That the situation of teachers must be made desirable by adequate compensation, by good treatment, by suitable accommodations, and by uniting his labors to the requirements of health and self-improvement."

This polite language reflected great educator dissatisfaction with conditions of work, outrageously low salaries, and overwork. This same convention saw the passage of a resolution calling for *merit* to be the main criteria used in employing teachers — instead of the favoritism that so often marred hiring and firing.

Professor
Alexander Crummell

1865

The Civil War and its consequences naturally preoccupied the group, and addresses were heard on coping with the impact of war on public education, the function of education in Reconstruction, and the urgent need to establish a federal department of education in order to provide and regulate education in the years ahead. The audience was addressed by a black American—Professor Crummel—who had been educated at Cambridge University in England, and had taught in Liberia for many years. His remarks stressed the need for improved education for all in the South after the war.

1866

The spirit of egalitarianism moved within NTA and members voted to change the Constitution to read that membership would be open to "persons," instead of the former "gentlemen." There was no need to alter the Constitution in regard to minority educators; there had never been any restrictions included.

1867

The NTA achieved a major objective when Congress created a Department of Education. The bill, lobbied by NTA, had been sponsored by Senator James A. Garfield of Ohio (he'd been an educator), and was signed into law by President Andrew Johnson on March 2, 1867. The perception of some, at the time and later, was that this new department, in a government still miscellaneously titling agencies "bureaus" and "departments" and "offices," was a creation entitling its chief executive a seat in the President's Cabinet. Henry Barnard, the first commissioner, later said that he knew when appointed that the position would not hold Cabinet rank, but the title "department" had been bestowed on the new agency to free it from control of other existing departments and to give it dignity and status. The stipulated purpose of the Department was to collect statistics, disseminate information and promote the cause of education throughout the country.

1868

Congressional concern about the new Education Department resulted in its summary demotion by title to the status of "bureau," and the Commissioner's salary was reduced. Over the objections of NTA and Senator Garfield, those Congressmen invoking the age-old fear of federal government domination were the ones who prevailed—and demotion carried the day. And so began the Association's hundred-year struggle to have education represented in the Cabinet of the United States government.

Until the 20th century, the school teacher was commonly expected to be a young, single person (no one was expected to support a family on a teacher's wages) either en route to a career or marriage.

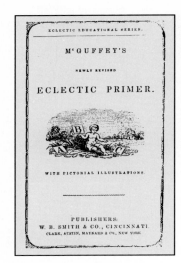

1869

Emily Rice became the first woman to be elected to national NTA office when she was chosen Association Vice-President.

1870's

The NTA became the "National Educational Association." This was done by the absorption of three other smaller organizations — the American Normal School Association, the National Association of School Superintendents, and the Central College Association. All three became NEA departments, and the Association created an additional new department to serve elementary education.

The 1870's most important educational development came in 1874, with the *Kalamazoo* decision by the Supreme Court. This decision, for once and all, made it clear that public funds could be used to pay for secondary schools. When the decision was handed down, the practice was well-established in some portions of the country, but was not universally accepted. This decision, and the ensuing upsurge in the creation of high schools nationwide, was central to the future of the schools. NEA applauded this decision, not only because it meant an open door to the expansion of public education, but because it eliminated one level of energy-consuming debate for educators everywhere.

Night school for working children, 1873.

The Froebel system of kindergarten—which offered specially designed games and play activities to encourage pre-school children to grow and blossom—was introduced to Americans at the Women's Building of the Centennial Exhibition in Philadelphia, 1876.

1880's

Thomas W. Bicknell

In 1881, a significant development occurred on behalf of the cause of education when Booker T. Washington founded Tuskegee Institute.

In 1883, Thomas W. Bicknell was president-elect of NEA. Bicknell, a nationally-known publisher of educational journals, a writer and educator, was deeply troubled by NEA's constant poverty and resulting inability to attract large numbers of new members.

Bicknell was committed to changing that. In 1883, he spent his personal monies travelling around the nation promoting the 1884 convention, to be held in Madison, Wisconsin. Bicknell was a natural organizer. Wherever he went, he met with the press, extolling the importance of NEA and the beauties of Madison, Wisconsin. He persuaded the press to spread the word, and he persuaded the railroads to offer extremely inexpensive discount rail fares to Madison—and to collect the $2.00 NEA dues from passengers on the train, and give the receipts to NEA! Bicknell also had the railroads help NEA by distributing 100,000 copies of a 16-page pamphlet on the organization and Madison, highlighting, of course, the cheap railway fares.

"The grandest and most numerous assemblage of educators that ever came together on the American continent." It worked. When the convention opened in Madison that summer, Bicknell was to preside over an audience of more than 5,000 educators—plus a number of other American and European citizens who'd come to see the show. Bicknell, of course, address the convention. He arose, "majestic, over six feet tall, straight as a ship's mast, with full beard, a bald strip running over the top of his head, two wisps of iron-gray hair standing out on the sides after the fashion of two horns, and with the voice of a Stentor."

At the heart of his remarks was a deep and abiding concern for the well-being of the profession: ". . .It is a high crime and misdemeanor of the state to ask us to expend our best energies in the instruction of our youth and then require us to use the balance in solving the problem of how to make the week's wages meet the week's necessary expenses."

Bicknell also announced that 54 percent of the delegates were women and that special access to opportunities to address the convention had been provided for them: ". . .the large opportunity granted to women at the present meeting may be regarded as confession and penance for past shortcomings."

When membership soared to over 2,800, the Association was out of the doldrums.

Schools were expected to be the agents of acculturation and assimilation, as immigrants streamed into the country during the 19th century. "The Education of the Mongolian or Chinese" was the topic of a speech presented to the 1896 convention.

Certificate of Incorporation
issued in Washington, D.C.,
on February 23, 1886.

Certificate of Incorporation of the } Recorded February 24th 1886 4 P.M.
National Education Association }

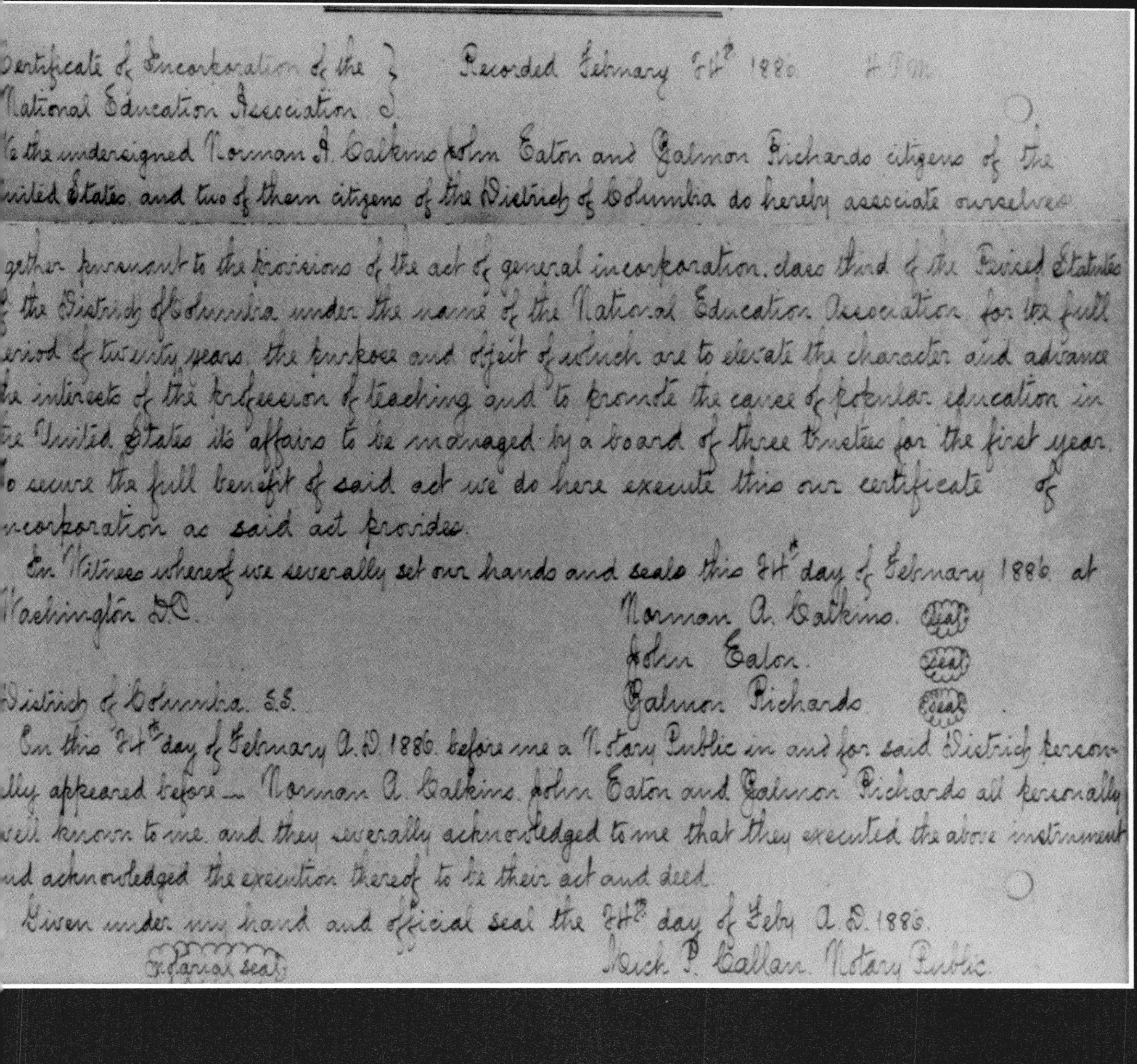

We the undersigned Norman A. Calkins John Eaton and Zalmon Richards citizens of the United States and two of them citizens of the District of Columbia do hereby associate ourselves together pursuant to the provisions of the act of general incorporation class third of the Revised Statutes of the District of Columbia under the name of the National Education Association for the full period of twenty years the purpose and object of which are to elevate the character and advance the interests of the profession of teaching and to promote the cause of popular education in the United States its affairs to be managed by a board of three trustees for the first year. To secure the full benefit of said act we do here execute this our certificate of incorporation as said act provides.

In Witness whereof we severally set our hands and seals this 24th day of February 1886 at Washington D.C.

Norman A. Calkins (seal)
John Eaton (seal)
Zalmon Richards (seal)

District of Columbia S.S.

On this 24th day of February A.D. 1886 before me a Notary Public in and for said District personally appeared before — Norman A. Calkins John Eaton and Zalmon Richards all personally well known to me and they severally acknowledged to me that they executed the above instrument and acknowledged the execution thereof to be their act and deed.

Given under my hand and official seal the 24th day of Feby A.D. 1886.

(Notarial seal)

Mich P. Callan Notary Public.

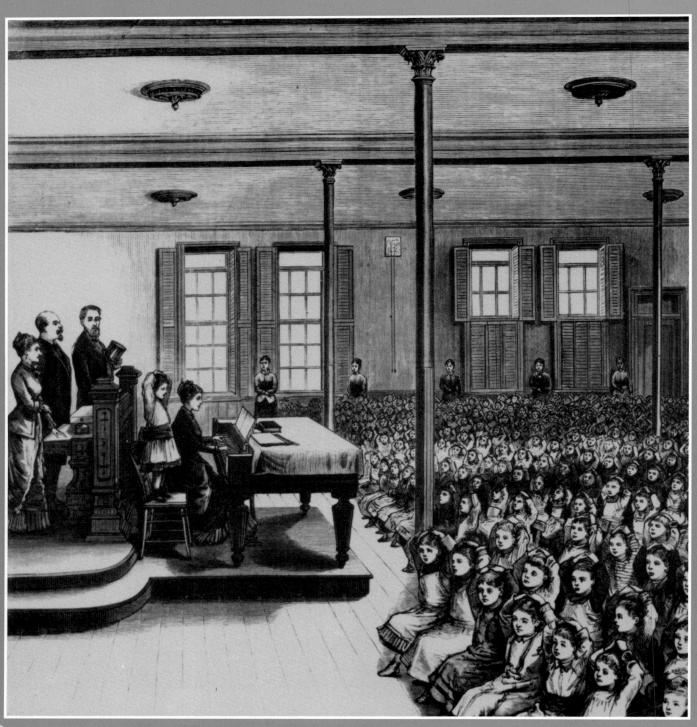

An exhibition of calis-
thenic exercises, 1881.
Physical and health
education made their
appearance early in
the 1900's.

THE NATIONAL COUNCIL ON EDUCATION

The National Council on Education, created from an idea of Bicknell's in 1881, began as a part of NEA intended to "reach and disseminate correct thinking on educational questions." What was wanted here was a body, attached to but separate from NEA, that would serve as a fount of the best thinking educators could muster on developing educational questions, a group unrestrained by the need to adhere to any one school of thought, any given ideology. Nineteenth-century educators, it must be remembered, still believed that sufficient intellectual exchange would ultimately produce wisdom and unity. The Council, composed of fifty-one members chosen by the five Departments of NEA and the NEA Board, was from this point on reflective of those in positions of educational leadership — professors, superintendents, educational writers, administrators. Its members perceived the Council's pronouncements as "correct thinking," and believed that what it communicated would be received as advice from "a wise parent."

For a time, its members served as perhaps the nation's most important group of educational leaders, and they produced exhaustive reports on many critical topics such as teacher licensure, opportunities for educating the rural population, the need for educational research and the collection of statistics, and so on. From 1885 to its demise in the 1940s, the roster of Council members included the names of most leading American educators. These men and women also were responsible for much of the educational content of NEA conventions for many years, creating programs and debates on an enormous range of topics.

In 1886, the American Federation of Labor was formed, the creation of twenty-five craft unions. NEA, already twenty-nine years old, had matured enough to name a Board of Trustees to oversee the Association's Permanent Fund. 1887 saw the NEA calling for the creation of retirement plans for teachers in each state; none existed at the time.

A manual training class in Holyoke, Massachusetts. NEA published its *Report of Committee on Hindrances and Helps to Manual Training in Industrial Education* in 1898.

In 1896, the United States Supreme Court, in *Plessy v. Ferguson,* upheld legal segregation of public schools, perpetrating the damaging and retarding "separate but equal" concept. This forced black teachers into a desperate struggle to try to provide those "equal" resources for the black children they taught — a struggle that, in 1904, would cause the creation of the "National Colored Teachers Association"—which soon changed its name to the "National Association of Teachers in Colored Schools," in order to avoid the appearance of excluding white teachers teaching in black schools.

In 1898, NEA could afford a full-time staff member to order the Association's growing business. Elected to the position was Irwin Shepard, of Winona, Minnesota.

Shepard had been serving as a part-time executive secretary for a number of years, and had been successful at his labors. He was paid a salary of $4,000, and elected for a given number of years, much like the Association's other officers. Headquarters would be in Shepard's home in Winona.

Finding qualified black teachers in rural communities was a problem after the Civil War—blacks with a good education usually left their rural communities in the South for the opportunities available in northern cities.

Women in the teaching profession—"Schoolmarms"—achieved more autonomy, acceptability and self-sufficiency than practically any other group of women in the 19th century. This was often sacrificed, however, upon the decision to wed—many states had laws barring married teachers.

TURN-OF-THE-CENTURY AMERICA
1900-1925

High school senior class, 1899.

OFFICIAL PROGRAM

National Educational Association

National
Council of
Education,
July 8 and 9

National
Educational
Association,
July 9 to 12

Fortieth Annual Convention
Detroit, Mich.,
July 8 to 12, 1901.

As a new century began, teachers still weren't making much progress. Salaries still remained under $50 a month in most locales, and women were usually still paid less than men. Further, when salary increases came, they came primarily to secondary school teachers at the expense of those teaching younger children. This helped drive more and more women from the teaching ranks into industry jobs.

This produced some new developments within NEA. At the 1903 convention in Boston, fiery Margaret Haley, an NEA member and leader of the Chicago Federation of Teachers, led a demonstration to bring attention to the need for improvement of the lot of teachers. This demonstration produced a call for funds to be appropriated by NEA to work to improve teacher salaries, tenure and pensions. It was done: NEA created the National Committee on Salaries, Tenure of Office and Pensions of Teachers. This Committee, in 1905, produced a massive 466-page report to the profession and to the American people on the conditions of employment in public education. This document recorded the pay of teachers in nearly all cities larger than 8,000—and went on to suggest ways that more public funds could be raised to produce higher salaries. Clearly, this began NEA's continuing primacy as the best source of financial and statistical information and analysis of public education and public school employees — a primacy that is unchallenged today.

J.R.E. Lee

Other events of importance marked early twentieth-century Association activity. J.R.E. Lee, a prominent black educator, made a call to teachers in black schools throughout the nation, and the Association that became *The National Association of Teachers in Colored Schools* was founded in 1904. Lee, who served as director of the Academic Department of Tuskegee Institute and later as president of Florida A&M University, was NATCS president until 1909, and remained a lifelong advocate of educator involvement in professional associations.

In Illinois in 1904, the Saline County Teachers Association appointed a committee to study salaries, which was done by also studying the revenues available to the county government with which to pay teachers. The Association then drew up a salary schedule calling for minimum salaries from $25 to $100 per month and mailed it to every teacher in the county, asking them not to sign contracts for work unless the schedule was honored. The school committee was most displeased—but the teachers had captured the public's support—and the schedule was enacted when it became clear that the majority of teachers would not sign until the Association's demands were met. One hundred and twenty-five teachers, *organized*, had improved their situation.

In 1906, NEA was incorporated by an Act of Congress, and President Theodore Roosevelt signed the Charter. On June 30, 1906, NEA officially became "The National Education Association of the United States."

Ella Flagg Young, first woman president of NEA.

NEA AT FIFTY

In 1907, when NEA celebrated fifty years of existence, membership had reached 5,044. Internal debate preoccupied the Association, as classroom teachers pushed harder for a greater voice within the Association, and a greater voice in making educational decisions where they worked. For the NEA's first fifty years, administrators had led the organization. Now, as teachers increasingly dominated the membership population, they were no longer content to be led. Ella Flagg Young, superintendent of Chicago, destined to become NEA's first woman president, told NEA in this year: "If the public school system is to meet the demands which 20th century civilization would lay upon it, the isolation of the great body of teachers from the administration of the school must be overcome. . . .can it be true that teachers are stronger in their work when they have no voice in planning of great issues committed to their hands?"

First NEA Headquarters, Winona, Minnesota, 1907.

In 1910, in convention at Boston, a major victory came for the Association's "progressives" when *Ella Flagg Young* was nominated for president of NEA from the floor of the convention, and defeated the candidate selected by the nominating committee. Her policies and positions on inclusion of teachers at every level of school decision making brought fresh air and new ideas to the Association and helped dissipate the growing conflicts within NEA.

Other events were helping to improve circumstances for teachers. In 1909, due to the efforts of the New Jersey Education Association, *the nation's first tenure law was enacted.* In 1911, NEA's Committee on Salaries, Tenure and Pensions, distressed by the absence of public school system retirement plans throughout the nation, began to inform the public of this situation — and the drive to establish such systems began.

First official NEA seal, designed by Frank D. Millet, adopted in 1909.

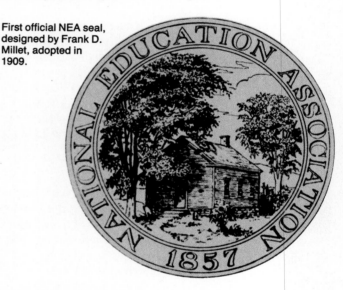

In 1912, NEA formally endorsed women's suffrage, and the Association's Commission on the Reorganization of Secondary Education began its work. This group issued bulletins for years, recommended appropriate curriculum changes, and worked closely with the United States Bureau of Education in getting the word out nationwide on the best approaches to high school education.

Our children they grow up unlearned
No time to go to school;
Almost before they've learned to walk
They learn to spin or spool.

The boss man jerks them round and round
and whistles very keen;
I'll tell you what, the factory kids
are really treated mean.

"Let Them Wear Their Watches Fine"—a song transcribed by Will Geer from the singing of a woman in the mountains of West Virginia.

(Taken from *American Folksongs of Protest*, by John Greenway. Perpetua Books, A.S. Barnes and Co., Inc., N.Y. Copyright 1953, University of Pennsylvania Press. Perpetua Edition 1960.)

In 1917, the NEA
moved its Headquar-
ters to 1400 Massa-
chusetts Avenue,
Washington, D.C.

1913 saw the creation of NEA's *Department of Classroom Teachers*. This department, created to hurry the pace of progress in improving the welfare of teachers, did not accept the notion that the building of the profession should take precedence over the achievement of status and dignity for classroom teachers. DCT became, as the years passed, a natural training ground for many who would come to lead NEA, and did much to bring women in the Association into greater prominence. Additionally, DCT launched immediately into activism on behalf of classroom teachers, calling at once for the creation of teacher advisory councils to give professional and expert advice to school boards and administrators; calling for an end to ''arbitrary and perfunctory'' teacher evaluation systems; and pushing hard for salary improvements, tenure creation and pension plans to keep good teachers in the profession. As one educational leader, A.E. Winship, stated, ''There will be no democracy in education that does not come to and through and by the classroom teacher.'' Until the group decided to disband in the 1970's—because *all* of NEA existed to serve teachers— DCT (later the Association of Classroom Teachers) served as an eloquent and effective voice for the growing role of classroom teachers inside the NEA and within school districts throughout the nation. All classroom teachers were automatically considered members of DCT, and the organization's mission proceeded with a clarity unique in Association activity of the times.

Official Program

Fifty-second Annual Convention

NATIONAL EDUCATION ASSOCIATION

ST. PAUL, MINNESOTA JULY 4th to 11th, 1914

1913 brought the birth of the *NEA Bulletin*—forerunner of the *NEA Journal*, and, later, *Today's Education*. Finally, NEA had a professional journal, a vehicle through which all members and a larger public audience could learn of NEA's vision for public education. The 1914 Convention went on record reaffirming a commitment to equality: ''The Association . . .declares itself in favor of the political equality of the sexes and equal pay for equal services.''

In 1917, the NEA moved to Washington, D.C., there to establish a permanent headquarters. *James W. Crabtree* became the NEA's Executive Secretary at this time, and declared his goal to be ''100 percent membership in local, state and national associations with every teacher at work on the problems of the profession.'' In 1917, the average teacher's annual salary was approximately $640 and, with the declaration of war, many of those who were not in the armed forces left teaching for more profitable work in industry.

1917, too, was the year in which NEA began the practice of alternating the Association's presidency between men and women. NEA also was to play a role in helping with the war effort, organizing the teaching profession's campaign for food conservation, and developing education programs for our soldiers.

James W. Crabtree was NEA's Executive Secretary from 1917 to 1935.

In 1918, NEA's Commission on the Reorganization of Secondary Education issued the "Cardinal Principles of Secondary Education."

These principles are said to have influenced the direction of public schools more than any other single statement of these years and people quickly realized that the principles applied to the goals of *all* education, not merely the secondary level. The principles live on today. As recently as 1966, NEA Research asked members in a representative survey if the Principles, as listed below, still reflected the goals of education; 85 percent said that they did.

CARDINAL PRINCIPLES OF SECONDARY EDUCATION

1. *Health and safety;*
2. *Worthy home membership;*
3. *Mastery of the tools, technique and spirit of learning;*
4. *Citizenship and world goodwill;*
5. *Vocational and economic effectiveness;*
6. *Wise use of leisure;*
7. *Ethical character.*

In 1918, NEA membership finally topped 10,000. Teachers in Memphis, Tennessee went on strike, demanding a significant pay increase; the School Board made an acceptable offer, and the strike was settled.

NEA's *Commission on the Emergency in Education* was formed to make recommendations on how the nation should handle teacher shortages that were growing in intensity throughout the nation, as a result of higher salaries being offered in industry. The Commission surveyed school districts throughout the country, and in 1919 published *Teacher Salaries and Salary Schedules in the United States* — a major publication that included an analysis of the salary situation of teachers and proposals for salary schedules that would do much to retain career teachers.

Women's vocational
training, 1919.

GOING TO THE PEOPLE

NEA realized that if any significant changes were to be forthcoming, public attitudes about teachers and public schooling required vigorous attention. Therefore, the members of the Commission on the Emergency in Public Education journeyed to more than thirty states in 1919-20, seeking and securing newspaper coverage for their message, which was that salaries must be raised at once, and that standards for teacher qualification should also be raised. The message worked; it was communicated to community leaders, businessmen, bankers and farmers, to clubwomen and to labor organizations: "Pay the teachers!" The Chair of the Commission, Joseph Swain, who had served as NEA President in 1914, spoke bluntly: "Education is a national matter. . . . .The man who denies education is capable of denying that our army and navy are national matters, of thinking that our states and towns and cities, left to themselves, could carry on the War. . . .But suppose a nation cannot be made to see its duty. Then there is only one other way: the teachers, by concerted action and the application of the principles of collective bargaining, must compel the nation to wake up."

NEA introduced a bill in Congress based on this report, calling for the creation of a Department of Education, for funds to reduce illiteracy, programs for the Americanization of immigrants, for teacher training, and for the equalization of school opportunity for all children. NEA had, in 1919, reaffirmed by resolution the call for a department, headed by a Secretary of Education seated in the President's Cabinet. NEA's concern for a means to assist education on a national level increased as a result of the investigations conducted by the Emergency Commission. These investigations revealed alarming levels of illiteracy in American soldiers and neglect of new immigrants to the nation, who urgently needed special educational treatment to assimilate and become productive citizens. But the bill was not to pass. The opponents of any and all federal aid to education argued, yet again, that "federal aid means federal control."

Joseph Swain

The Guggenheim Mansion at 1201 16th Street in Washington, D.C. was purchased by NEA in 1919 for $98,000. This site remains NEA's home today, though nothing remains but the mantelpiece in the State Dining Room.

NEA was also working for other important national goals in 1919, voting support for the League of Nations and for passage of a child labor law to protect children from abuse. The child labor amendment finally passed Congress in 1924, but was never ratified by enough states to become law. Many states enacted their own laws on this matter, and, despite the pressure from NEA and other concerned groups over the years, no national legislation was enacted until 1941, when the United States Supreme Court, overturning an earlier decision of the Court made in 1917, ruled that the first federal child labor law (the Child Labor Act of 1916) was constitutional.

Teacher pensions—the absence of them—continued to preoccupy NEA, and in 1919 the Committee on Salaries, Tenure and Pensions issued a major report detailing the need for pension programs and describing ways in which states could establish such plans. *In 1919, New Jersey became the first state to enact pension legislation.* Without question, NEA's detailed report and suggestions were central to many states' decisions to create retirement plans for teachers that would help attract qualified people to the profession and keep them in for a career.

In the 1920's NEA encompassed 39 employees, 5 divisions, 17 committees, 2 commissions, 20 departments, 49 state Associations, 522 local Associations, 75,000 members, and a budget of $140,000.

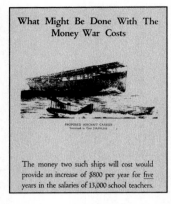

What Might Be Done With The Money War Costs

PROPOSED AIRCRAFT CARRIER

The money two such ships will cost would provide an increase of $800 per year for five years in the salaries of 13,000 school teachers.

1920 was a dramatic year in American history. The Senate refused to ratify the League of Nations charter, shattering President Wilson's hope for the best means to prevent future wars; Sacco and Vanzetti were arrested, and the "Red Scare" sweeping the nation resulted in the arrest of more than 2,700 accused communists and anarchists. Women's suffrage finally became the law of the land, after years of effort to enact it.

In this year, the National Education Association changed from a convention organization to a *Representative Assembly,* in which the conduct of Association matters and the creation of policy would be done by a body— the Representative Assembly—composed of delegates from affiliated states and locals, rather than by those who happened to turn up at any given convention. This also meant that officers would be elected by the Representative Assembly by ballot. By now, the state Associations had approximately 300,000 members, and were achieving a level of strength and stability that made them representative of large numbers of teachers. NEA had grown too large to be run on an ad-hoc basis, responsive only to those who attended the annual meeting and run the rest of the time by a small group of leaders. Democratization was needed and was the purpose of the change, which made direct connections between the national and the state and local Associations possible.

It was an idea whose time had come; by 1921, when the structure formally took effect, forty-four state Associations had affiliated, as well as four hundred sixty-three locals. There was interest in having locals affiliate with states, and then having states affiliate with the national— but the idea didn't catch fire because at this time unified membership was nothing more than a glimmer in Executive Secretary Crabtree's eye; no one had to join all three levels of the Association, and not many chose to do so. Therefore, it was decided to permit membership at a variety of levels, depending on individual choice — and affiliation had to follow a similar pattern to conform to the thinking of the times.

Welcome to the NEA

American Education Week was initiated by the Joint Committee of NEA and the American Legion.

A Petition for a Department of Education

To the President of the United States:

On behalf of our respective organizations we earnestly pray that in the reorganization of the Executive Departments of the Government, education be given recognition commensurate with its supreme importance to the Nation. The purpose of public education is to develop good citizens. Since the citizenship of our Nation is but the aggregate citizenship of the States, the Nation is and always must be vitally interested in education.

If the Federal Government is to perform its proper function in the promotion of education, the department at Washington must be given such dignity and prominence as will command the respect of the public and merit the confidence of the educational forces of the country. The educational leader of the Nation should hold an outstanding position, with powers and responsibilities clearly defined, subordinate to no one except the President.

In view of the reorganization now pending, the present is a most opportune time for giving education its proper place in the Administrative Branch of the Government. On behalf of the National organizations which we represent, each of which has officially taken action in accordance with the prayer of this petition, we respectfully urge that the President of the United States use his great influence to bring about the creation of a Department of Education with a Secretary in the Cabinet.

Respectfully submitted,

President of the National Education Association

President of the General Federation of Women's Clubs

President of the National Committee for a Department of Education

President of the National Society of the Daughters of the American Revolution

President of the American Federation of Labor

President of the National Congress of Mothers and Parent-Teacher Associations

Director of the American Council on Education

President of the National Council of Jewish Women

President of the American Library Association

President of the Woman's Relief Corps

President of the National Federation of Musical Clubs

President of the Woman's Christian Temperance Union

Sovereign Grand Commander of the Supreme Council, Scottish Rite of Freemasonry, Southern Jurisdiction of the United States

Chairman of the Committee on Education of the Sunday School Council of Evangelical Denominations and the International Sunday School Association

OCTOBER, 1921

JANUARY, 1921   NO. 1

The JOURNAL of the NATIONAL EDUCATION ASSOCIATION

A Platform of Service—An Editorial 1
A National Program for Education 5
Editorials 8
Educational Opinion 9
The Educational Advance 10
Teacher Situation—City Schools 11
Campaign for Education in Ohio 13
Enrolment and Affiliation 14
Notes and Announcements 15
Department of Superintendence—Program . . 16

Published monthly, except July and August, by the
NATIONAL EDUCATION ASSOCIATION OF THE UNITED STATES
1201 SIXTEENTH STREET NORTHWEST, WASHINGTON, D. C.

First issue of the *Journal*, January 1921.

1921 brought the creation of *American Education Week*, a coalition of NEA, the American Legion and the U.S. Office of Education. The Coalition's purpose was to generate more public attention to the importance of public education. The American Legion involvement arose from the shocking statistics emerging from World War I, in which it was discovered that 25 percent of the soldiers were illiterate and 29 percent were physically unfit to fight. Also in 1921, a petition to the President of the United States was presented, urging the creation of a cabinet-level Department of Education. Signers included, besides NEA leaders: Samuel Gompers, President of AFL, the Sovereign Grand Commander of the Masons, the president of the Women's Temperance Union, the president of the Parents-Teachers Association, the American Library Association, the Daughters of the American Revolution and the American Council on Education. The effort was a failure; no bill was enacted.

In 1923, NEA played a central role in establishing the first international group for educators in helping to found the "World Federation of Education Associations." It began some years before when the President of Czechoslovakia suggested that NEA sponsor a world conference on education. NEA liked the idea, and arranged for President Harding to extend invitations to other countries to send delegates. About fifty nations accepted. The meeting, held in San Francisco, offered sessions on topics such as world health, international ideals, the dissemination of educational information and rural education.

In 1924, NEA's Higher Education department withdrew from the Association because this group found itself in substantial disagreement with NEA's growing preoccupation with the wartime economic problems of elementary and secondary teachers. This preoccupation —fueled by difficulties in achieving appropriate salaries and other protections for members—was eased somewhat by the publication of *The Fundamental Principles of a Teacher Retirement System,* which rapidly became the most respected authority on what should be included in a workable teacher retirement program. The publication inspired many states to establish reasonable teacher retirement programs in the years ahead.

WORKING TOGETHER
1926-1934

An event occurred in 1926 and a tradition began that would be central to reshaping and expanding the mission and scope of the National Education Association for generations to come. In this year, *the first joint committee of NEA and the National Association of Teachers in Colored Schools was formed.*

The NATCS had come to NEA for assistance with a problem that was thwarting educational improvement in the South, as teachers there struggled to cope with "separate but equal" education for black students. The Southern Association of Schools and Colleges had refused for years to evaluate and accredit schools for black children—and this was effectively blocking students from acceptance in many colleges and universities, since they were forced to graduate from nonaccredited schools. NEA agreed to assist, and the Joint Committee supported the ongoing massive efforts at persuasion underway by NATCS. Eventually, the SASC began the process of evaluating and accrediting black schools.

However, it was clear to NATCS and NEA that this step was a long way from producing all that black educators wanted and needed for their schools. Therefore, NEA and NATCS decided to make the Joint Committee a permanent one to work for improvement in all areas of education. This Committee existed until the two organizations merged in 1966. Much was accomplished in the ensuing forty years of cooperation. Surveys and research studies were conducted on the special problems involving black education; the Associations worked with publishers to have unbiased textbooks produced, ones that featured minority accomplishments and contributions to the nation; NEA actively worked to involve minorities more effectively in policy-making levels of the Association; many, many conferences and workshops were held on the principles of human relations, and prominent black educators were featured speakers and guests at NEA conventions. The Joint Committee also worked with Congress and federal agencies on programs to provide federal assistance for equalizing educational opportunities, and both organizations worked to help establish training centers for doctors, dentists and nurses to serve blacks.

Emmett J. Scott and Booker T. Washington.

On October 29, 1929, the Stock Market crashed—and the nation's and world's economy became everyone's immediate preoccupation.

NEA saw that the schools were brutally impacted by the Depression. Tax-cut fever swept the country, and schools were an immediate target. Many districts found themselves so financially devastated, as tax revenues dissipated, that they were unable to pay their teachers, and many schools were forced to close altogether. There assuredly was no money for materials and supplies, and teachers in some instances were forced to copy texts longhand to make enough for students to use. Former supporters of education—notably politicians—could no longer be counted upon to speak up on behalf of quality education and teachers.

The work of NEA was more important now than ever. The second *Commission on the Emergency in Education* was created, and the Commission immediately set about collecting information about what was happening to the nation's public schools. The Commission members visited schools throughout the country, and as they went, they worked with newspapers, magazines and radio to disseminate the information and get public attention focused on the problems. NEA, as never before, was in the forefront of protecting the interests of members and of the children in the public schools.

When Franklin Roosevelt took office in 1933, the nation—and its public schools were a shambles. Immediately the Federal Advisory Committee on the Emergency in Education was created, representing thirty-two national organizations, including the NEA. This massive group formulated a six-point plan for improving the schools, and the end result was a respectable amount of federal aid for rural schools, adult education, nursery schools, school building repairs and construction. Needy college students were able to get assistance as well.

Progress was significant and badly needed assistance finally began reaching the schools.

A 1927 first grade class at work on projects.

Willard E. Givens,
NEA Executive Secretary, 1935-1952.

In 1934, NEA membership stood at 160,883, and more than 5,000 schools had 100 percent membership.

In 1935, NEA created the *Educational Policies Commission.* It had no policy-making function within NEA, and was free to make wide-ranging surveys and public pronouncements as it saw fit. Charged with the task to "prepare, publish and disseminate...statements of proposed policy regarding the conduct of education in the United States, and the international relationships of American education," the members of the EPC were prestigious enough to command respect nationwide. This group, originally created to last only five years, went on to affect the development of public education for more than thirty years, speaking freely and openly on what members considered important educational questions.

Willard Givens was selected as Executive Secretary in 1935, and Congress enacted the National Labor Relations Act, providing a structure and regulations for private sector workers. Public employees, such as teachers, were excluded from coverage by the NLRA—an omission that, with the advent of collective bargaining for education employees and other public workers in later years, would cause considerable and unfortunate confusion. Also in this year, Congress enacted Social Security–and again teachers and many other public workers were excluded.

ACADEMIC FREEDOM: THE STRUGGLE CONTINUES 1935-1949

A first grader receiving special attention from the teacher, 1938.

In 1935, a rider—"the little red rider"—was attached to a Congressional appropriations bill for the District of Columbia public schools. This rider provided that no employee of the schools could receive his or her paycheck without swearing an oath that he or she did not teach nor advocate communism. The implications of this blatant loyalty-oath legislation were clear—and extraordinarily oppressive and ominous for teachers. NEA immediately denounced this first attempt by Congress to censor education and demean educators, and led the charge on efforts to have the rider repealed. Editorial support was gained from newspapers, and other organizations joined in protesting this harassing legislation. Finally, in 1937, the rider was repealed.

In 1941, the United States entered World War II. NEA played an active role in the nation's war effort, coordinating registration for the draft and for the rationing of sugar, oil and canned goods, promoting the sale of Defense Savings Stamps and Defense Bonds in the schools, and encouraging school children to salvage scrap metal and plant "victory gardens."

NEA in this year was successful in passing the *Lanham Act* through Congress, generating special federal funding for public schools in the areas of military bases and other federal installations. This relieved local districts of the burden of financing the education of the many thousand children of families at such installations which did not add to the local area's tax base. "Impact aid" has become an important revenue source for such school districts, and NEA continues to lobby to keep the assistance part of the federal budget.

In 1941, NEA created the important *Commission on the Defense of Democracy Through Education.* Donald DuShane was president of NEA in this year and he was deeply committed to the defense and protection of the rights of all educators. The Defense Commission was his creation, and it existed to investigate violations of members' rights, whenever and wherever they occurred.

Other accomplishments of this Commission included the establishment of local defense committees, and campaigning for increased salaries for teachers. Other concerns included child labor and teacher shortages, and, because of one particularly ugly case, the urgent need for tenure laws throughout the nation.

Donald DuShane, 1941 NEA President, created the Commission on the Defense of Democracy Through Education to investigate violations of members' rights. Today's Kate Frank/DuShane Fund is named in DuShane's honor.

THE KATE FRANK CASE

This case, to be of lasting importance to educators nationwide, involved the firing of three teachers in Muskogee, Oklahoma without warning or opportunity for hearing. Kate Frank was one of the three, and she chose to stand and fight back, with NEA's help. She had been fired because she was an Association activist who, on behalf of teachers, had been in conflict with the school board and had helped organize an effort to unseat several board members in an election in 1942. NEA's Defense Commission and the Committee on Tenure saw this as a basic test of a member's right to free speech, and persuaded the Executive Committee to allocate $10,000 for her defense. The case was finally won and Frank reinstated in 1945. $948.39 remained after all bills were paid and this became the *Dushane Fund for Teacher Rights,* named after President DuShane who had created the Defense Commission. Recently the Fund was renamed the *Kate Frank/DuShane Fund*—and it remains today the school employee member's single most potent weapon to ensure that rights cannot be exploited for lack of legal defense.

The Defense Commission fought the good fight on a wide range of issues, in many locales throughout the country—academic freedom, censorship of libraries and textbooks, racial discrimination. It published a regular bulletin, "True Faith and Allegiance," specifically on racial discrimination problems. Commission investigations attained the reputation of highly principled actions, and this helped the Commission secure many important victories for teachers, including basic rights to notification of performance problems, notice of impending discharge, an opportunity to reply to charges in a public setting, and the right of appeal. The Commission's activities—and its mission—can best be summed up by a memorable statement made by one of its distinguished chairmen, Harold Benjamin:

"Free men cannot be taught properly by slaves; courageous citizens cannot be well educated by scared hired men."

The *Hatch Act* had passed Congress, prohibiting federal employees from certain political activities—and it was interpreted as applying to teachers as well, those whose programs received any funds whatsoever from the federal govenment. The Commission led a coordinated struggle of all three levels of the Association to fight this, and in 1942 the Act was revised and teachers were specifically excluded from coverage.

Kate Frank

WHAT Makes an AMERICAN ?

Courtesy, WRA

Left—Tenth-grade students at the Rohwer Relocation Center, McGehee, Arkansas. Right—A typical nissei family—Bill, Alice, and Mike Koskokowa. Bill is editor of the Sentinel, Heart Mountain Relocation Center newspaper.

WILLARD W. BEATTY
Director of Education, U. S. Office of Indian Affairs

THE NEW EMERGENCY *raises many problems of justice and wisdom, not the least among them the rights and principles involved in removing from their homes a large number of United States citizens of Japanese ancestry. This project undertaken in the heat of excitement following Pearl Harbor is now being reviewed in the light of less pressing circumstances.*

FEW Americans realize that between seventy and eighty thousand American citizens are today under "protective custody" of their government in primitive camps, surrounded by barbed wire fences, and guarded by armed troops. Fantastic as it may seem, these citizens are not charged with being party to any crime, and their loyalty to the United States has been pretty clearly established. It is not even certain that the restraint which has been imposed upon them is legal under the Constitution. The basic cause of this un-

American discrimination is that these Americans have the misfortune to have had ancestors born in Japan.

America is today the home of countless citizens who were born in Germany and in Italy—as well as in lesser countries affiliated with the Axis. Their loyalty and that of their children is taken for granted, unless overt acts indicate otherwise. How does it happen that we have acted differently toward our citizens of Japanese ancestry? And is our action consistent with American democracy?

At the outbreak of the war, there were approximately 130,000 persons of Japanese ancestry in the United States—a trifling number in comparison to most of our racial groups, and fewer than the number of "enemy aliens" from Italy. About 37 percent of this Japanese group has been born in Japan and most of these are more than fifty years old. They are called "issei" or "first generationists." The rest were all born in the United States, and with the exception of a small number have been brought up and edu-

cated in this country. They are called "nissei" or "second generationists." A few of these were sent back to Japan to be educated, and then returned to America. They are referred to as "kibei."

A limited number of the entire group, engaged in fishing, were to be found living adjacent to military or naval installations along the Pacific coast. Many people believed that this proximity was deliberate and for subversive reasons. Following Pearl Harbor there was a demand for their removal, which was expanded by anti-Japanese groups in the Western states which have long been jealous of the economic success of the Japanese, into pressure for the removal of the whole population of Japanese ancestry from their homes. In response to this pressure, there was issued on February 19, 1942, an executive order authorizing the Secretary of War to prescribe "military areas from which any or all persons may be excluded."

The west coast was then divided into two military areas, one embracing the coastal strip, the second the valley areas

---

In 1943, the Representative Assembly chose to make an important viewpoint clear and passed a New Business Item: *"Be it resolved that in choosing the city for conven-* *tions, the National Education Association shall see to it that only those cities shall be selected where it is possible to make provisions without discrimination for the hous-* *ing, feeding, seating at the convention, and general welfare of all delegates and teachers, regardless of race, color or creed."*

In 1944, NEA helped pass the *G.I. Bill* for education returning soldiers-but the Association was disappointed to see that funds for the Bill's implementation were distributed outside the auspices of the U.S. Office of Education. Mistrust of a federal role in education hadn't diminished much—and each time something of this nature occurred, NEA's dream of a cabinet-level Department of Education seemed farther away.

Eleanor Roosevelt visits with NEA officials after her address to Headquarters staff on "The Role of the Educator," January 21, 1944.

In 1945, fifty nations signed the Charter creating the United Nations—and NEA played a role in this. Association leaders and representatives from other concerned organizations were instrumental in securing specific recognition for education in the United Nations Charter, and NEA to the present time has been involved in United Nations matters of concern.

International issues continued to be important to NEA, and in 1945 the Association began organizing a World Conference on the Education Profession, to be held as soon as world travel conditions permitted.

And in this year all but one state had established retirement programs for teachers; less than one percent of the nation's 870,000 educators had no retirement protection.

NEA's TEPS Commission—*Teacher Education and Professional Standards*—was created in 1946, taking as its challenge the words of *NEA Journal* editor Joy Elmer Morgan: "It is not possible for society to guarantee to every child a devoted mother and a wise, provident father, but society can guarantee to every child a competent, well-prepared and adequately-paid teacher." TEPS was pledged to influence the acceptance of only the finest candidates into teacher training, certification requirements of four years of college, ongoing professional growth opportunities for teachers in practice, adequate provision for teacher welfare, and the general professionalization of the profession. Its work was successful, in large measure. From 1946 to 1955 the professional standards for teachers improved. In 1946, only fifteen states required a degree for elementary school teachers; by 1955, thirty-five states required it. In 1946, only 41,000 degree-holding teachers were trained. The number in 1955 was 86,000. In 1946, only 45 percent of elementary teachers had a degree; 68 percent did in 1955. In 1946, only 72 percent of teachers had tenure of some sort available; 82 percent did in 1955. In 1946, 340,000 teachers belonged to NEA—and in 1957, the number exceeded 700,000.

An Association strike for a contract—the first ever—came in 1946, when NEA's *Norwalk Teachers Association,* frustrated and unhappy with conditions, struck until the School Board agreed to sign a written contract. This effort helped pass a law in Connecticut several years later which gave teachers bargaining rights and mediation procedures when agreement could not be reached.

By 1947, sixty percent of teachers were college graduates. However, many of the remaining forty percent were teaching on emergency certificates, issued during the massive teacher shortage during the War years.

1947 brought the affiliation of 18 southern black state teachers Associations with NEA. While blacks had been welcomed as full members in NEA since the Association's founding in 1857, and while black educators in other areas of the country that did not separately educate black and white children had traditionally been members of NEA's state and local Associations there, the South in these years presented a different problem. There, by custom and at times by statute, blacks and whites weren't members of the same organizations. NEA's affiliation strategy of the late 1940's was an attempt to include greater numbers of Southern black educators through the state affiliates of ATA.

THE FIFTIES
YEARS OF PROGRESS

One of many fund raising efforts by state affiliates to collect money to build the NEA Headquarters. Pictured is a booth at the Georgia convention in 1953.

The 1950's brought 33 million students to the nation's public schools. They also brought Senator Joe Mc-Carthy, the first test of the hydrogen bomb, Sputnik, statehood for Alaska and Hawaii, and increasing attention nationwide to the problems of equal justice for minorities in public facilities and in public schools.

The first military advisers were sent to South Vietnam; the Rosenbergs were convicted of conspiracy to commit wartime espionage, and the Korean Conflict came to an end. Rosa Parks refused to give her seat to a white man on a public bus in Montgomery, Alabama, and a United States Federal Court found segregation ordinances of this sort unconstitutional. An anticommunist revolution was thwarted in Hungary, and the first domestic jet airline passenger service was inaugurated, from New York to Miami.

In 1952, NEA helped create the *World Confederation of Organizations of the Teaching Profession* (WCOTP). This body of international educators, now representing 85 nations, has worked since the 1950's to improve the quality of education throughout the world and especially to defend educators' individual and collective rights.

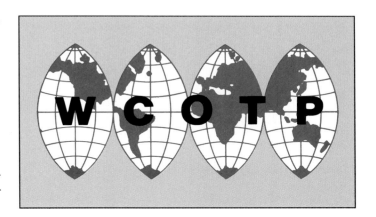

Dr. William G. Carr became executive secretary of NEA in 1952 and in this year NEA began work on the $5 million headquarters building that is the Association's present home. The Department of Health, Education and Welfare (HEW) was created by the Eisenhower Administration, dashing yet again NEA's hope for the creation of a separate cabi-net-level Department of Education.

NEA published "Salary Schedule Provisions on Salaries Paid in Degree-Granting Institutions, 1952-53," becoming the first national organization to conduct a national survey of faculty salaries and salary schedules. Later, in 1955-56, NEA performed the same service for junior colleges.

NEA Headquarters.

BROWN V. BOARD OF EDUCATION

Brown v. Board of Education. This United States Supreme Court decision, handed down in 1954, was without question the single most important event impacting public education in the decade—and its impact continues today. The decision, ordering the desegregation of the nation's public schools, put an end to the doctrine of "separate but equal" established in 1896 in *Plessy v. Ferguson*.

Also in 1954, NEA, with the American Association of Colleges of Teacher Education, the National School Boards Association and the National Association of State Directors of Teacher Education, founded NCATE—the *National Council for Accreditation of Teacher Education*. This new organization was largely the creature of NEA Teacher Education and Professional Standards (TEPS),

and was created to improve teacher education by standardizing the accreditation for teacher training programs, by accrediting programs and annually publishing a list of those programs that had been accredited, and by having NCATE's member organizations do whatever possible in their purview to improve teacher education.

Black And White

The ink is black,
the page is white,
Together we learn to read
and write, to read and write.
And now a child can
understand
This is the law of all the
land, all the land.

Their robes were black, their
heads were white,
The school house doors were
closed so tight,
were closed so tight.
Nine judges all that signed
their names
To end the years and years of
shame, years of shame.

A child is black,
a child is white,
The whole world looks upon
the sight,
the beautiful sight,
For very well the whole
world knows
This is the way that freedom
grows, freedom grows.

(traditional)

58

THE CENTENNIAL YEAR–
1957

In this year, NEA had 703,800 members. Decisions were made by a Representative Assembly of 5,000, a seventy-seven-member Board of Directors, an Executive Committee of eleven, twelve vice-presidents, a treasurer, a president elected for a one-year term and an executive secretary. NEA had grown to include thirty departments, twenty-one of which resided within the NEA Headquarters.

NEA held its Representative Assembly in Philadelphia in the summer of 1957—the city where it all began one hundred years earlier. The centennial history book was presented, and a highlight of the celebration included President Eisenhower cutting an enormous birthday cake, an event carried to other Association gatherings throughout the country on closed-circuit television.

The Association's first one hundred years, in retrospect, reveal an organization struggling to strengthen public education in the United States. NEA had been primarily concerned with making the profession more respected and improving the credentials of educators. Protection and advancement of individual rights rested mainly with the state Associations at this time. In the 1940's and 1950's NEA had increasingly found itself speaking out to the public on behalf of education's and educators' problems and needs—and this had made the organization more appealing to teachers, who began to join in increasingly larger numbers. The membership figure of 1957 was the highest in Association history.

In 1958, the *National Defense Education Act* (NDEA) was funded by Congress, providing significant new federal funds for the improvement of education in science, mathematics, and foreign language study. The new law, backed by NEA as a viable way to improve education, also offered National Defense funds for college students studying in these disciplines.

In 1959, Wisconsin became the first state to enact a *collective bargaining law* for public employees, including teachers. This law, the first of many to come in the 1960's and 70's, would help usher in an era of teacher bargaining that would transform the Association.

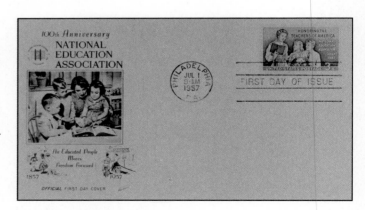

Cachet and stamp issued to honor the 100th Anniversary of the NEA in 1957.

U.S. President Dwight
D. Eisenhower stayed
to cut the cake after
his speech at the NEA
Birthday Party, 1957.

THE SIXTIES:
DECADE OF GROWTH AND CHANGE

The decade began with the American U-2 plane shot down over the Soviet Union, and closed with 250,000 Americans gathered in Washington, D.C. calling for a moratorium in Vietnam, protesting the involvement of 543,000 American soldiers there. It was a decade of social unrest, change and trauma. Sit-ins occurred in the South, John Glenn became the first American in orbit, the Berlin Wall was erected to keep the East German people in, and James Meredith became the first black student at the University of Mississippi. Martin Luther King, Jr. spoke to an enormous crowd at the March on Washington for Civil Rights, saying, ''I have a dream that this nation will rise up and live out the true meaning of its creed, 'We hold these truths to be self-evident: that all men are created equal.''' King was awarded the Nobel Peace Prize, and was assassinated before the decade closed. Also assassinated were President John F. Kennedy and his brother, Robert Kennedy; three civil rights workers were murdered in Mississippi. The United States Supreme Court found that recitation of the Lord's Prayer or Bible verses in public schools was unconstitutional, and the Congress finally passed the Civil Rights Act, giving all persons access to all public facilities.

Thurgood Marshall became the first black ever to sit on the United States Supreme Court. In 1968 thousands of the nation's youth gathered in Woodstock, New York, for the nation's largest celebration of music and youth.

It was a decade of tremendous social change and unrest in the United States—a decade of violence, and a decade of anger. Millions were discontent with the way things were and struggled to change them, to make a better world in which more rights were accorded to more people. NEA members were directly involved in the struggle for a better world.

U.S. President John F. Kennedy talks to Association officials on November 19, 1963. NEA President Bob Wyatt is at the President's left.

1962

In this year the Representative Assembly, acting by resolution, called upon school boards to recognize the right of teachers to be represented by the Association in determining wages and working conditions, and

NEA CONVENTION 1962

to develop mutually acceptable procedures to resolve problems. The resolution called for the creation of state laws for this purpose. With this action, NEA's push for collective bargaining was fully institutionalized.

1963

By 1963, more than one million copies of NEA's "Guidelines for Professional Negotiations" had been issued to locals everywhere. NEA's new Urban Services Project was growing rapidly, and, through the resources of the Department of Classroom Teachers, bargaining seminars were being offered and conducted for local Association leaders. NEA "Salary Schools" were regularly attended, and did much to ensure that representatives of teachers at the bargaining table were prepared to represent members successfully.

1964

By 1964, 100,000 teachers in 346 school districts were working under written agreements—and NEA locals were the bargaining representative in the overwhelming majority of these districts.

In this same year, the United States Congress passed the U.S. Civil Rights Act, ensuring all persons the right to be served in public facilities. In 1964, NEA saw the case of teacher Willa Johnson all the way to the Supreme Court. Johnson had been fired because of her leadership in her area's voter registration drive. NEA bore the costs of litigation, and provided Johnson funds to live on during the struggle. She was awarded reinstatement to her position as well as damages. The Court found that teachers hold sensitive jobs and their rights should receive special protection.

*It isn't nice to block the doorway, it
isn't nice to go to jail,
There are nicer ways to do it but the
nice ways always fail,
It isn't nice, it isn't nice, I told you once,
I told you twice,
But if that's freedom's price, we don't mind. . .
no, no, no, no, no, we don't mind.*

from "It Isn't Nice"
by Malvina Reynolds

Here's ONE NATIVE SELMIAN for FREEDOM and JUSTICE

An NEA staff reporter covered the historic civil rights march from Selma to Montgomery, Alabama, in 1965 to provide national coverage for the Selma Teachers Association.

In April 1965, President Johnson signed into law the Elementary & Secondary Education Act, providing $1.2 billion for public schools—the first massive infusion of federal dollars for the nation's schools.

1965

NEA helped in a voter registration drive for black teachers that was to have impact beyond the campaign itself. The teachers in Selma, Alabama organized a campaign to register black educators, called ''Fit to Teach, Fit to Vote.'' NEA provided financial support for this effort, and the leaders of both the NEA and the American Teachers Association visited the campaign to help. The teacher leader of the campaign, Fred Reese, went on to become chair of the Selma Improvement Association, the group with whom Martin Luther King, Jr. worked in establishing the right for all blacks in Selma to vote later that year.

The Elementary and Secondary Education Act was signed into law in April 1965 by President Lyndon B. Johnson, and represented the first truly massive infusion of federal funds for the public schools. NEA played a critical role in passage of this landmark legislation, by helping draft the bill's language, by intensive lobbying, by bringing hundreds of people to Washington to testify, and through back-home lobbying of Members of Congress. The bill provided $1.2 billion for schools, and distributed funds to the states based on the numbers of children in low-income families. Education was seen as the brightest hope for the poor, a mechanism through which one could escape the bonds of poverty. President Johnson had been both a student and a teacher in one-room schools in Texas, and felt close to the problems educators faced. He came to the 1965 Representative Assembly, and in his remarks to the group called the legislation ''the broadest, most meaningful and most sweeping federal commitment to education that this nation had ever made.'' NEA agreed, and presented this former teacher with a special honorary life membership in NEA—a gesture of deep appreciation for his support from the nation's grateful educators.

1966

In 1966, the process which had begun with talks in 1963 bore fruit, and both the American Teachers Association and the National Education Association voted approval for merging the two organizations.

The ratification vote at NEA was unanimous, and every state Association demanded the privilege of seconding the motion for merger. The Unification Certificate was signed by the presidents and executive secretaries of both organizations, while delegates sang ''Glory, Glory, Hallelujah.'' A prolonged standing ovation followed the signing.

In the years ahead, those states still having separate black and white Associations merged them. By 1977, all state Associations had merged.

At the first Human Rights Banquet in 1967, H. Councill Trenholm Awards were given to Hudson Barksdale of South Carolina and Irvamae Applegate of Minnesota, for their leadership in human rights.

Merger agreement between the American Teachers Association and the National Education Association was signed at formal ceremonies at the Miami Beach convention in 1966.

In 1967, NEA became a million-member organization. The Association honored Donald Harris of California and the half-millionth member, Eloise Pendarvis of South Carolina.

1968

In 1968, largely because of NEA lobbying efforts for three years, Congress passed the *Bilingual Education Act*, mandating that all school districts with sizable populations of Spanish-speaking students provide special programs for those students' education. Federal funds were provided for those programs, including teacher training and materials. The push for enactment of federal assistance to students of this kind began at an NEA-sponsored conference in Tucson, Arizona in 1965, "The Spanish-Speaking Child in the Schools of the Southwest." Conference members concluded that such children were not deficient learners but rather victims of inappropriate materials, undertrained educators and poor techniques available to remedy their situation. Since the Act's passage in 1968, NEA has consistently worked to increase federal funds for this important program.

Elizabeth Duncan Koontz of North Carolina became the first black president of NEA in 1968.

In 1968, the United States Supreme Court, ruling in *Maryland v. Wirtz*, held that the Fair Labor Standards Act applied to certain employees of public institutions, including schools, and did not infringe on states' rights under the 10th Amendment to the Constitution. In sustaining a lower court's ruling in this case, the Court noted that the Fair Labor Standards Act was a valid exercise of Congressional power under the Commerce Clause. This paved the way for an effort to secure federal collective bargaining legislation for public employees. NEA and other groups immediately accelerated plans to achieve passage of such a law. However, the 1976 *League of Cities* decision by the Supreme Court essentially reversed *Maryland v. Wirtz*—and dampened efforts by public employee groups like NEA to secure bargaining legislation. NEA has continued to pursue other constitutional avenues for the achievement of legislation. A recent Supreme Court ruling in *Garcia v. San Antonio* has offered new hope, as this finding reports that the 1976 *League of Cities* decision "was not only unworkable but. . .inconsistent with established principles of federalism." NEA and other public employee organizations continue to pursue a federal collective bargaining law; private sector workers have enjoyed the legal right to bargain for more than fifty years.

1969

In 1969, the NEA Executive Committee launched the Association into the forefront of rights activities and political action, when it voted to publicly oppose the nomination of Clement F. Haynesworth to the U.S. Supreme Court: "Judge Haynesworth's record on civil rights renders him unfit to hold this high position." This same verdict was levied on the nomination of Judge Harrold Carswell in early 1970.

Dr. Sam M. Lambert served as NEA Executive Secretary from 1967 to 1972.

By 1969, 43% of school systems enrolling 1000 or more pupils had some sort of negotiations agreement with teachers—and the National Education Association local affiliates were the chosen representative in 92% of these districts. Teachers covered in these systems numbered more than one million.

There were 171 teacher strikes in 1969, the majority of them caused by school districts' refusal to permit educators to share in local decision-making.

35,000 Florida teachers, frustrated and angry at the state government's refusal to adequately fund public education, gathered in the state's Tangerine Bowl to protest. In 1968, 26,000 Florida teachers went on strike, and NEA provided $2 million in interest-free loans to help the strikers. Teachers throughout the country, at NEA's request, contributed a day's pay to help the Florida teachers

THE SEVENTIES: AFFIRMATIVE ACTION & POLITICAL ACTIVISM

It was a stressful and difficult decade for America. For the first time, a seated President of the United States resigned his position in disgrace; and for the first time, many Americans believed that the nation had lost a war. "Double-digit" inflation became a catchphrase in the headlines. Other bad news dominated the headlines as well—Kent State, Three-Mile Island, Patty Hearst, Gary Gilmore, Proposition 13, and Watergate. As the decade ended, an exhausted nation witnessed one of the country's largest automobile manufacturers requiring a $1.5 billion federal government loan to survive, and the capture of 63 Americans at the United States Embassy in Teheran by Iran's hostile anti-American zealots.

In all, NEA thrived in the Seventies. A new Constitution brought beneficial internal restructuring; membership grew; and significant new legislation aiding students and educators was enacted. Members of NEA everywhere learned, for once and all, that almost all educational decisions are in some way political decisions, and charted a new course for the Association that has done much to further aspirations and improvements for schools and the profession. Program services were expanded to reach out to the local Association level. New coalitions were formed. By paying close attention to the needs and desires of members, NEA in the 1970's continued to be an organization moving steadily forward.

1970

UniServ begins. In 1970, NEA raised dues to $25.00—for the times, enough for growth—and the nationwide UniServ (Unified Service) program was instituted to provide high-quality staff assistance to local Associations as they struggled with collective bargaining, defense of member rights, political action, and many other matters. Based on the ratio of approximately one professional staffer for every 1200 members, this program continues to be of invaluable assistance to school employees in building and maintaining strong local Associations.

In 1970, the Association's minority caucuses were formed, and NEA's Minority Involvement Program began. MIPs have been held throughout the country, and served as a viable means for bringing more minority group members into greater activism at all levels of the organization.

Members of the Oklahoma Education Association Human and Civil Rights Committee meet in 1973.

1970 saw NEA's deep involvement in efforts to help make school desegreation work. When thirty school districts in Mississippi were ordered to desegregate at once, teachers in the state saw that there would be a major problem and secured assistance from NEA. NEA's immediate response was the formation of a twenty-five person *Mississippi Task Force*, which went at once to the state to collect data on events there, work with state and federal agencies as well as Association members, secure public attention to the problems and injustices, and coordinate with other groups like NAACP and the American Civil Liberties Union. The state government fought back, and over time, NEA representatives were served with 19 separate injunctions to block investigations. The Task Force persevered, and reported that white parents were withdrawing their children from public schools and creating private ones; that in some cases public facilities were being used to house these private schools; that black educators were being fired, demoted or pressured to resign from the desegregating districts; and that several public schools were burned to the ground to prevent integration from occurring in them. NEA provided legal help for educators fighting discrimination,

bringing court actions in local districts and at the state capitol; took legal action to prevent the sale or transfer of public school property, equipment and materials; and blocked the state from giving financial assistance to private schools. NEA also worked for a compulsory school attendance law, and reported findings to the United States Government.

In February 1970, again the news was bad for black educators, this time in Louisiana. NEA dispatched a second Task Force, which found that half the schools in the state were desegregating, but still major patterns of discrimination against blacks were evident. Many white students were being removed from the public schools, and habitually many districts forced black principals to accept lesser positions in desegregated schools. Once again, NEA provided legal help and staff assistance for these educators, and com-

municated Task Force findings to the Mondale Committee on Equal Educational Opportunity. These findings influenced the forthcoming Emergency School Assistance Act.

A third Task Force visited Mississippi and Louisiana in the fall of 1970, and reported findings in a news conference in New Orleans. The patterns were becoming predictable: demotion and dismissal of black educators done by a variety of devices, including the misuse of the National Teachers Exam; unfair treatment of minority students, including segregated classes in "desegregated" schools; separate lunch and dismissal times for black and white students, and more. Some progress had been made, however, in some areas of these states, and NEA was able to report that positive growing influences of the state and local Associations were being felt.

Association of Class-
room Teachers-ACT
Forum first meetings
were held in 1972.
These meetings were
the beginning of the
Minority Leadership
Training Program.

The Association negotiated the first collective bargaining agreement at a four-year institution of higher education in 1970, when the faculty Association at Central Michigan University secured average raises of 12 percent and a meaningful role in decision making.

Legal defense for higher education members continued to be a critical need in the 1970's. The precedential *Roth* and *Sinderman* cases (heard at the same time by the Supreme Court) were decided. The Court ruled that no faculty member could be nonrenewed because he or she chose to exercise a constitutional right, and that due process must be given to any faculty member, regardless of tenure status, when charges were made that could damage the individual's personal or professional standing. By 1974, the NEA Du-Shane Fund had litigated or provided assistance in 115 separate college and university lawsuits involving faculty members.

1971

The 26th Amendment to the Constitution was enacted, lowering the voting age to 18 in federal, state and local elections. NEA had worked for passage of the Amendment as an expression of the Association's belief in expanding the rights of individuals and groups in American society.

NEA Constitutional Convention at Fort Collins, Colorado, 1971.

1972

NEA and the Equal Rights Amendment. In 1972, ERA had passed Congress and was sent to the states for ratification. NEA gave immediate support for the Amendment, and, in 1975, the Representative Assembly voted not to hold NEA Conventions in any state that had not ratified ERA. NEA's Annual Meeting is one of the nation's largest, bringing more than 10,000 people to the city designated each year; refusal to meet in states where the Amendment had not been ratified was a significant effort in terms of economic pressure. In 1977, the Representative Assembly voted to refuse endorsement to any political candidate failing to support ERA, and, in 1980, NEA employed full-time staff to coordinate the national and state drives for passage. This drive for ratification of ERA failed—but when ERA is again passed by Congress, it is certain that NEA will once again be at the forefront of the ratification campaign.

ERA America held its kickoff news conference at NEA Headquarters.

Dollars for Higher Education. In 1972, a $20 million higher-education bill fostered by NEA was passed, providing significant new revenue for colleges and universities.

NEA-PAC. In 1972, mechanisms for the operation of a national Political Action Committee, NEA-PAC, were put in place. Initial contributions were raised for federal candidates for office who were favorable to public education, and what was to become one of the nation's largest and most influential PACs was up and running. The 1972 Representative Assembly directed the Association leaders and staff to develop a procedure for endorsing a candidate for the office of President of the United States, authorized a $1.00 voluntary contribution for political action in addition to dues, and directed the NEA Board to attend to all necessary details to see that NEA-PAC complied with federal regulations. In this first year, NEA-PAC supported 32 candidates for federal office, and 26 were victorious.

Thousands of NEA members across the nation helped elect friends of education by participating in telephone banks and other campaign activities.

In 1972, NEA affiliates represented members in 3891 school systems of a total of 3911 engaging in collective bargaining.

1973

A New Constitution. As NEA had grown, and as more and more classroom teachers formed the majority of the Association membership, the call for a more open and accessible organization became imperative. Efforts to devise a new governing document began at NEA's Constitutional Convention (CON-CON) in Fort Collins, Colorado in 1971 and ended in 1973 when the new Constitution was approved by the Representative Assembly, to take effect in 1975.

It was determined that local Associations would decide on the composition of each local affiliate, and with-

in NEA, classroom teachers and administrators would be entitled to proportional representation in the Representative Assembly and the Board of Directors. The officers of NEA would serve for a two-

Terry Herndon served as NEA Executive Director from 1973 to 1983.

year term with the right to one more two-year term if reelected. The President of NEA would be the primary Association spokesperson, and the position of Executive Secretary became that of Executive Director, with responsibility to employ staff, consult with the leadership, speak for the Association on matters of policy or at the discretion of the President, and administer the budget of NEA.

Minorities would be represented on the Board, Executive Committee and Association committees in numbers no less than 20 percent. Minority representation in the

RA, from each state, would reflect the proportion of minorities present in the state's overall population. Other adjustments included the creation of a Review Board, with jurisdiction over alleged violations of the Code of Ethics, and other alleged professional misconduct; secret ballot elections and open nominations must be the practice for the election of all representatives to the NEA; and the requirement that all affiliates require members to belong to the local, state and national levels of the Association. Unified membership was fully realized in the 1975-76 year.

At the heart of the sweeping and energizing policy changes that were encompassed in the new Constitution was a desire by those who comprised the overwhelming majority of the Association's membership to direct the destiny of that Association.

Classroom teachers predominated in NEA, but until the new Constitution became reality, the voice of this vast majority had not always been heard in the shaping of policies and practices.

The new Constitution presents a portrait of an organization committed to the empowerment of the voices of its members in decision making, as well as to an effective operation. The rights of individual members are protected and honored through such provisions as open nominations, secret ballot elections and one-person, one-vote requirements for affiliate governing bodies.

The Coalition of American Public Employees was formed by NEA and the American Federation of State, County and Municipal Employees (AFSCME), AFL-CIO in order for these two organizations and other interested groups and unions to work closely together to improve conditions for public workers. Many of AFSCME's and NEA's views on the needs of public employees were similar; both organizations are deeply committed to the attainment of a federal collective bargaining law for public workers.

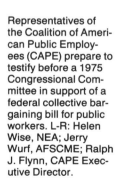

Representatives of the Coalition of American Public Employees (CAPE) prepare to testify before a 1975 Congressional Committee in support of a federal collective bargaining bill for public workers. L-R: Helen Wise, NEA; Jerry Wurf, AFSCME; Ralph J. Flynn, CAPE Executive Director.

NEA AND ORGANIZED LABOR

Merger with AFT. Before the 1970's, several attempts had been made to entice NEA into merger with the American Federation of Teachers, AFL-CIO. A new attempt was launched in 1972, when Albert Shanker, president of the United Federation of Teachers in New York City and aspirant for the presidency of AFT, persuaded the New York State Teachers Association to merge with UFT, forming NYSUT—the New York State United Teachers. In this same year, an NEA member poll showed that 61 percent of the Association's members would quit NEA if the Association merged with AFT, AFL-CIO. The 1972 Representative Assembly passed a new business item stipulating that ''In the future, NEA and its affiliates will not enter into a merger requiring affiliation with the AFL-CIO,'' but the body did authorize NEA representatives to engage in merger discussions with AFT, to see if any workable compromise could be found. While some Association leaders believed that AFT's interest in merger was sincere, most believed that AFT was trying to accomplish by merger that which had proven impossible by persuasion. AFT's efforts to raid Association membership city by city and town by town had been largely a failure, underscored in 1971 by the Federation's failure to capture an entire state—Hawaii—in a bitterly contested representation election. Merger talks began in 1973. NEA representatives were President Helen Wise and Executive Director Terry Herndon; AFT was represented by UFT President Al Shanker and AFT President David Selden. NEA insisted on three critical conditions:

1. Teachers would not be required to belong to AFL-CIO;
2. The Association's minority guarantees in the Constitution would be retained;
3. All elections would be conducted by secret ballot.

AFT rejected all three criteria, and talks broke off in February, 1974.

The 1982 policy of NEA, adopted by the Board of Directors, does encourage productive relations with organized labor. While the Association assuredly will continue to pursue the organizing of faculties and all other school employees with vigor, and while the numerous defects of AFT will continue to receive attention and publicity from NEA, the Association does not believe that the Federation's faults are the result of its membership in AFL-CIO. NEA believes that the labor movement is an important and valuable part of American society and continues to support the organizing of workers and the legitimate demands of trade unions. NEA plans to continue an expanding partnership with the AFL-CIO, seeking alliances and working relationships that are of mutual benefit.

1974

An end to mandatory maternity leave for teachers came in 1974 in an NEA-backed case heard before the United States Supreme Court. The Court found that such regulations, perpetrated on thousands of female teachers over the years, "employ irrefutable presumptions that penalize a female for deciding to bear a child." NEA had spent more than $25,000 to achieve this precedential and welcomed ruling, representing Jo Carol LaFleur, Elizabeth Nelson and Susan Cohen.

Presidential Endorsement Procedure. In 1974, the Representative Assembly adopted the Association's Presidential Endorsement Procedure, to be used in 1976. Without question, the impetus behind this decision was years of frustrating effort to increase federal contribution levels to public education, as well as the damage done to the federal role in education during the Nixon and Ford presidencies. The Nixon years saw continuous impounding of funds authorized for education, and President Ford vetoed billions of dollars worth of legislation for educational appropriations, Head Start and school lunch programs. NEA and other groups were successful in overturning the Ford vetoes—but educators everywhere were fed up with the need to expend such extraordinary amounts of time and energy simply to maintain the status quo.

1975

In 1975, Public Law 94-142, the Education for All Handicapped Children Act, passed. NEA, while not entirely satisfied with the law (provisions for teacher training were inadequate), had worked for passage as a step in the right direction in enabling many handicapped children to attend public schools.

1976

Copyright Law changed for the better for educators in 1976, with the passage of legislation enabling limited duplication of copyrighted materials for teaching and research purposes. NEA had lobbied successfully for passage of this legislation.

An important change benefitting educators came with the improvements of *unemployment compensation provisions*, extending mandatory unemployment compensation coverage to all state and local public employees, and extended emergency unemployment compensation coverage of teachers and other public workers.

Commemorative stamp honoring collective bargaining (1976).

UNITED STATES
collective bargaining
out of conflict...accord
10c

Educational
strategies
during an
economic
crisis

nea
113th ANNUAL MEETING
LOS ANGELES, CALIFORNIA
JULY 3-8, 1975

NEA's first presidential endorsement took place in 1976, when delegates to the Representative Assembly voted overwhelmingly to endorse the candidacies of Jimmy Carter and Walter Mondale for President and Vice-President of the United States. Carter and Mondale were elected, and NEA's maiden voyage into presidential politics was successful.

In 1976, NEA endorsed 323 House candidates and another 26 seeking election to the Senate. 83 percent were elected. Records since these early years have reflected success rates as good or better. At the heart of NEA's success in political action is the growing number of local Association political action efforts, and the increasing number of members who are politically active. NEA-PAC contributions have also grown substantially, and this PAC stands today as one of the nation's largest and most successful because Association contributions come voluntarily from the grassroots members and reflect a brand of commitment that is backed by local and state level savvy and activism.

In 1976, NEA endorsed the successful candidacies of Jimmy Carter and Walter Mondale. NEA President John Ryor and Executive Director Terry Herndon present the candidates to Association leaders and staff at NEA Headquarters.

1977

In 1977, *teacher centers*, authorized earlier, finally received $75 million from Congress to get the centers established. Teacher centers were created to enable educators to deal with their own self-designed programs for professional improvement; the Centers were designed and run by educators, for educators. NEA had drafted the legislation for the centers, and worked for passage of the legislation and subsequent appropriations of funds.

The Social Security Amendments of 1977 adjusted the tax schedule to protect the long-term solvency of Social Security, requiring the Department of Health and Welfare to recommend language changes to eliminate sex discrimination, and prevented mandatory coverage of all public employees. NEA represented educator interests in lobbying for passage of these amendments.

1978

Significant legislation for schools and educators was enacted in 1978. The *Middle-Income Student Assistance Act* extended benefits of educational grants and student loan programs to middle-income students, while assuring that the most needy would also receive enough aid to pursue an education. The *Pregnancy Disability Amendment to Title VII of the Civil Rights Act* prohibited sex discrimination on the basis of pregnancy; and the *Energy Emergency Aid Act* provided $900 million for energy conservation grants to schools and hospitals. NEA worked for passage of all three laws.

NJEA's Quality Education Task Force worked to improve the state's instructional program.

NEA lobbying victories further the cause of education and educational employees.

Also in 1978, *Proposition 13*, a massive property-tax slashing initiative, passed in California—and inaugurated a wave of "tax reform" legislation and voter initiatives throughout the nation. Prop 13 cut California property taxes by an astonishing 57 percent—and presented an abiding threat to the quality of all social services provided by state government, including the public schools. NEA worked closely with state affiliates throughout the nation to help defeat such measures in whatever form they appeared, and spoke out vigorously for responsible budgets and rational tax measures in states and at the federal level of government.

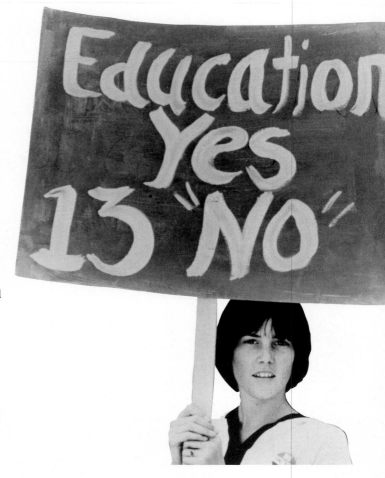

1979

Landrum-Griffin. Significant change came to NEA in 1979, when the Association was required, by the provisions of the federal Labor Management and Reporting Act (Landrum-Griffin) to

abolish specific minority representation guarantees in the Association Constitution for those elected to the Representative Assembly and other national offices. The NEA, already in compliance with

other Landrum-Griffin requirements, set about complying with this aspect of federal law—and did so with a renewed if unwritten commitment on the part of all levels of the Association to maintain the percentages of minority representation in governance levels that the Constitution had stipulated before the required amendments were made. That commitment—to have minority representation on governance bodies reflect their presence in the United States population—has been met in every year except one since 1979.

A SEAT AT THE TABLE: THE DEPARTMENT OF EDUCATION

U.S. President Jimmy Carter signed the bill to establish the United States Department of Education on October 17, 1979.

On October 17, 1979, President Jimmy Carter signed into law a bill establishing a cabinet-level Department of Education—and one of NEA's major legislative goals for the nation's schools was realized after more than one hundred years of effort.

NEA had long contended that the subsuming of education in a department with Health and Welfare worked against a meaningful federal role in public education. In the year before the creation of the Department, there were more than 40 federal agencies and bureaus managing about 200 different programs. This bizarre structure produced uncoordinated, unfocused efforts to help schools, and a sea of regulations that frustrated state and local school officials attempting to provide federal programs to their schools and colleges.

Efforts to get the new Department created were underscored by a remarkable cohesion of support for it from many, many groups and organizations concerned with education. Notably absent was the AFT. *New Republic* magazine noted that a Senate aide had said, ". . .AFT is against having a department because NEA is for it."

Perhaps the most important ingredient in the passage of this significant legislation was the tremendous amount of grassroots lobbying that went on at the local level as educators and other concerned citizens made certain that their Congressional representatives understood the importance of voting for the new department. The tide of public opinion favored passage, and educators, especially Association members, can take pride in the success of the effort. NEA Executive Director Terry Herndon said at an Association gala celebrating the Department, ". . .our membership grew to realize that virtually every public action affecting our profession and our students is political in nature, that our destiny as an Association is inextricably tied to the quality and character and talent of those we choose to govern us."

Glow by Josef Albers USA 15c

Learning never ends

The U.S. Postal Service issued a special commemorative stamp celebrating the creation of the U.S. Department of Education.

NEA Vice-President Bernie Freitag, Executive Director Terry Herndon, First Lady Rosalyn Carter and NEA President Willard H. McGuire celebrate the successful passage of legislation authorizing the new Department.

THE EIGHTIES:
SHAPING THE FUTURE FOR EXCELLENCE

NEA, in 1980, sent 464 delegates and alternates to the Democratic National Convention, and 22 members to the Republican National Convention.

NEA President Willard
H. McGuire.

For the National Education Association, this decade thus far has been one of great interest in improving the quality of public education, dramatic increases in political capabilities, intense concern for the status and employment conditions of school workers, and a commitment to outward expansion of the Association's membership in educational support personnel, Higher Education and retired educators.

NEA understands the critical *interdependence* of all school employees, and this understanding is evident in activities and decisions of the 1980's. The logic is simple: the more frequently and the more skillfully the family of education works together, the more successful all will be in attaining mutual goals. The essential unity of purpose that has been the touchstone of NEA's history—the desire to improve the quality of public education—leads inevitably to an understanding that all in the education community are mandated to work together if genuine progress is to be made. NEA of the 1980's—under the leadership of presidents Willard McGuire and Mary Hatwood Futrell—is reinvigorated by its commitment to bring all in the education world together. NEA is the only organization in the nation capable and committed to this task.

A sense of interdependence has also brought the Association to renewed efforts in working with the communities of the nation to achieve much-needed school reforms. The wide-spread renewal of interest in school reform has been welcomed by NEA—and the Association has responded to this concern by preparing and presenting to the nation reasoned and responsible recommendations for improvement that reflect the best thinking of the nation's largest representative of educators.

1980

One of the decade's most important decisions was made by the NEA Representative Assembly in 1980 in voting to extend full membership rights to *educational support personnel*. This step was critical to unifying and strengthening the Association. ESP members were already the recipients of full membership rights in some states, and this Representative Assembly decision paved the way for many more state Associations to offer full membership.

NEA Educational Support Conference, 1981.

1981

In 1981, the Reagan Administration, through public pronouncements and through attempts to enact legislation in Congress, embraced the notion of permitting parents who send children to private schools to receive tuition tax credits. NEA and the majority of other organizations concerned with preserving and advancing the quality of public education opposed this scheme, and successfully blocked enabling legislation from passage. In each year following, the Reagan Administration has attempted to pass legislation of this nature—and NEA has continued to successfully prevent its passage.

NEA-ERA Equality Day in support of passage of the Equal Rights Amendment was celebrated on July 7, 1981 at the Representative Assembly in Minneapolis, Minnesota.

1982

In 1982, NEA embarked on a campaign to improve the quality of schools through the introduction in Congress of the *American Defense Education Act*. This Act, introduced in both Houses, called for a renewed federal commitment to instruction in science, mathematics, guidance counseling, foreign languages and the new technology. NEA's proposal was designed to redress the critical shortage in math and science teachers, and other key areas as well. Funding provisions called for placing monies from the federal government directly into the hands of local school districts and institutions of higher education, where the most critical needs can best be identified and corrected.

"Be it resolved that classroom teachers must be involved in the initial planning, changes in work load, and designing of appropriate research related to all aspects of any new technology of instruction; and teachers affected by this new technology must be provided with adequate staff development to monitor changes in the quality of instruction and curricular coordination."

NEA Resolutions, 1981

POLITICAL POWER
FOR EDUCATIONAL
EXCELLENCE

nea
NATIONAL EDUCATION ASSOCIATION
120TH ANNUAL MEETING, LOS ANGELES, CALIFORNIA
JULY 1-6, 1982

NEA's *Lobby-by-Mail* program, introduced in 1982, provided a computerized means for Association members to share their views with Congressional representatives on issues of key importance to the Association. The program, which required each participating member's prior approval, issue by issue, has been effective in making Association sentiments known quickly.

Freedom Hall, consecrated to the memory of Dr. Martin Luther King, Jr., was dedicated in Atlanta on January 15, 1982, Dr. King's birthday. NEA members contributed more than $100,000 to this institution, where archives on Dr. King are housed and where space is provided for social programs such as teaching reading skills to adults, skill training in nonviolence and conflict resolution.

1982 Resolution on Peace: The National Education Association recognizes the interdependence of all peoples and urges that the United States make every effort to strengthen the United Nations to make it a more effective instrument for world peace. . . . The Association urges its affiliates and members to implement its commitment to world peace founded on genuine respect for and understanding of individual and cultural diversity and to develop programs that promote the ideals of peace, freedom and human dignity. . . .

In 1982, NEA's affiliate, the Congress of Faculty Associations (CTA-NEA, the American Association of University Professors and the California State Employees Association) won what stands as the single most important representation election ever held in higher education. CFA was selected as the bargaining agent for more than 19,000 faculty on 19 California campuses, defeating the AFT.

In 1983, Congress voted to declare Dr. Martin Luther King, Jr.'s birthday a federal holiday, beginning in 1986. NEA had lobbied for many years for passage of this new and significant law honoring one of the nation's finest leaders.

In 1982, *Excellence in Our Schools, Teacher Education: An Action Plan* was approved by the NEA Representative Assembly. The plan, focused on an insistence on more rigorous standards and meaningful preparation for teachers entering the profession, rests on one central premise: the experts on teaching are teachers. Its goal is to enable practicing K-12 teachers to play a major decision-making role in the development of teacher education policies and curricula in each state.

NEA had taken the unprecedented action of defining the knowledge and skill base that should be expected of teachers, and the 71-page document serves as a valuable blueprint for excellence in teacher education.

The plan calls for:

• Rigorous college admission standards based on firm evidence of the applicant's potential success as a classroom teacher.

• Teacher training programs based on what seasoned practitioners deem necessary for effective teaching.

• Expanded opportunities for education students to apply their knowledge and skills to the real world of teaching.

• Credentials for teaching based not on any single criterion, but on a variety of measures of the graduate's ability to practice effectively.

• Autonomous state agencies, governed by teachers and other professional educators, with the power to approve teacher preparation programs and certify practitioners.

• Majority governance of those state agencies by K-12 teachers, nominated by the appropriate NEA state affiliate.

1983

In 1983, the Representative Assembly adopted an amendment to the Association Bylaws giving *NEA-Retired* status as a new affiliate, and redefined the Retired class of membership. Under the new Bylaw, all retired teachers, regardless of previous NEA membership, are eligible for membership. The Bylaw makes available retired life memberships, extends the right to vote, to hold elective positions within the NEA and to be counted toward representation entitlement for the NEA Board of Directors and the Representative Assembly. The intent of this new program, which is succeeding in dramatically increasing the ranks of retired members, was to avail those wishing continued Association activity a vehicle for doing so—as well as bringing additional strength to NEA and to the state affiliates.

NEA Resolution:
EXCELLENCE IN EDUCATION

Be it resolved that the NEA believes that the continued success of the United States as a participatory democracy and as a world leader is dependent upon a shared national, community and individual commitment to excellence in education. To that end, the Association reaffirms its support for the establishment and maintenance of high standards for teaching and learning.

Mary Hatwood Futrell, President of NEA, spoke to a crowd of more than 250,000 gathered in Washington, D.C. in 1983 to re-enact the 1963 civil rights "March on Washington." President Futrell addressed the audience "as a woman, a classroom teacher, a descendant of slaves and as leader of our nation's largest union."

Members of the NEA marched on September 19, 1981, in support of Solidarity Day to protest the Administration's proposed budget cuts in social and educational programs.

Accepting the award at the 1984 Representative Assembly, Stafford stated, "This award belongs as much to you, members of the teaching profession. . . .You deserve recognition for all of us in Congress and from every other member of our educational community for your efforts."

Stafford stressed that future educational improvements must focus on providing equal educational opportunity for all in the country: "It does no good to fix the ship of education if we are going to keep some of its potential passengers stranded on the dock as the ship pulls away."

NEA's Friend of Education Award, the Association's highest honor, went to Senator Robert T. Stafford of Vermont in 1984.

Stafford, a Republican nominated by the Vermont-NEA, chaired the Senate Subcommittee on Education, Arts and Humanities. He helped lead the congressional opposition to tuition tax credits and steadfastly opposed efforts to permit prayer in the public schools.

NEA Blue Ribbon Task Force on Educational Excellence, 1984.

Don Cameron became NEA's Executive Director in 1983.

The national debate on educational excellence was joined with vigor in April of 1983, when the Report of the National Commission on Excellence in Education was released by the federal government. The Commission report contained much with which NEA agreed—and its publication helped focus the country's attention on the myriad problems of education—underpaid staff, poor materials, discipline problems, and more. However, in late spring of 1983, President Reagan announced his personal partiality to "merit pay"—a scheme of rewarding some teachers more than others—and refocused much valuable attention on a minor issue while neglecting real needs such as the universal sentiment for paying all educators adequate salaries to stem the tide of those quitting the schools for jobs with better pay, more respect and much less stress.

As state Associations began working with their legislatures and governors back home to achieve decent educational reform programs, the NEA Representative Assembly determined that the wisest approach for the Association to take to make its positions clear on quality reform would be the preparation of a report to the nation on what educators believed to be the best approaches to school improvement. The RA created the *Blue Ribbon Task Force on Educational Excellence*, to have its work completed for presentation to the 1984 Representative Assembly.

1984

An Open Letter to America on Schools, Students and Tomorrow, the product of the Blue Ribbon Task Force and the Representative Assembly, proposes nothing short of a revolutionary overhaul of public education, and sets forth what NEA believes our schools should be, now and in the future. Almost every aspect of education is given attention—the quality of learning, discipline, appropriate and inappropriate use of standardized tests, educational rights for the handicapped, preschool, daycare, adult education, class size, paperwork, time to teach, appropriate training for teacher aspirants, fair evaluation practices, salaries, school management—and more. *An Open Letter* has received wide national distribution, and is also valuable to affiliates in working to achieve meaningful reforms at the state and local government levels.

In 1984, thirty years had passed since the historic Supreme Court decision in *Brown v. Board of Education*—and NEA celebrated the decision by reporting on successful school integration in three major cities—Seattle, Charlotte-Mecklenburg in North Carolina, and Austin, Texas. In all three cities, NEA affiliates had worked and continue to work to make sure that quality integrated education benefits all students.

POLITICS '84: NEA IS STRONGER, MORE CREDIBLE THAN EVER

- *363 NEA members were delegates or alternates to the Democratic National Convention—a larger representation than that of any other organization or union. And the 15-person DNC platform drafting committee had two NEA members in its number.*

- *30 Association members participated in the Republican National Convention. They worked to eliminate anti-public education planks from the GOP platform.*

- *In the 1983-84 election cycle, NEA-PAC raised $2.5 million to help elect pro-education candidates to federal office.*

- *NEA members successfully aided in the election of 238 friends of education in 1984.*

- *And in this election year, USA TODAY, the nationwide daily newspaper, conducted a poll on the impact of political endorsements made by various major groups of the voting public. Forty-five percent of those questioned said that an endorsement by NEA made them* more likely *to vote for that endorsed candidate. No other group used in the poll, including the Chamber of Commerce, AFL-CIO, NAACP or the Moral Majority achieved a favorable percentage higher than 25 percent.*

1985

EdNet, a nationwide satellite hookup, was broadcast for the first time to eleven state affiliates in 1984. Here, members of the NEA Executive Committee wait for the cameras to roll. (L to R) Pearl Mack, Jim Lewis, John Wilson, Roxanne Bradshaw, Mary Hatwood Futrell, Keith Geiger, Ed Foglia, Gary Obermeyer, Odetta Fujimori.

Educators and Citizens Reject the Radical Right

The Radical Right, in 1985, hadn't lessened its efforts one bit to both wither the quality of public education and decimate the power of the members of the National Education Association.

But 1985 wasn't a good year for these extremist groups.

In Hillsboro, Missouri, a small, highly vocal group of parents—egged on by ultra-conservative education critic Phyllis Schlafly—began making appearances at Hillsboro school board meetings, to protest a wide range of school programs and activities. These efforts at censoring routine educational activities continued for three school board meetings—and then the thoughtful citizens and educators began to fight back. Hillsboro teachers worked to get the support of the community, including area clergy—and soon, parents began wearing "Stand By Your Teacher" buttons. The issue was resolved at a board meeting in February 1985, when a large crowd of concerned parents and educators had the satisfaction of seeing the school board refuse to submit to the extremist group's demands.

The source of activities like this lies in a set of federal regulations written to enforce a federal statute, the Hatch Amendment. This law was originally intended, states sponsor Utah Senator Orrin Hatch, to "let parents decide whether or not to permit their children to be subject to research and demonstration projects, a component of which is psychological or psychiatric testing or treatment." But now, groups like Schlafly's Eagle Forum say the Amendment covers anything that can be described as "controversial materials." The new regulations allow parents to literally demand a federal investigation of their school district if they don't believe their complaints are being appropriately handled at the school district level.

NEA's Human & Civil Rights division has encouraged districts to be certain to have well-thought-out policies in place, policies covering such topics as the selection of teaching and learning materials, and a sound process to handle parent complaints.

In a recent Supreme Court decision involving the concept of exclusive representation in bargaining, *Minnesota State Board for Community Colleges v. Knight,* the court found that an exclusive bargaining agent had the right to represent faculty on issues within and outside the scope of bargaining. This case was launched by the National Right-to-Work Committee. The faculty was given legal support by the Minnesota Education Association and NEA for the Association's local affiliate, the Minnesota Community College Faculty Association, the exclusive bargaining agent for faculty in the state's 18 public community colleges.

And, determined to thwart the efforts of the Radical Right to roll back more than a century of work to protect and expand the rights of school employees and other public workers, NEA has begun extensive efforts to provide members and other interested persons with detailed information on the Radical Right, as well as information about all aspects of Association policies and positions. NEA believes that the time has come to take the offense against these groups and their financial and organizational backers, as they present a threat to the survival of public education.

NINE PRINCIPLES OF EDUCATION

In 1985, the NEA Representative Assembly embraced the *Nine Principles of Education* to guide the Association, in regard to effective schools for the future.

Principle One:
Students must master what is taught. The objective of education should be a demonstrated grasp of fundamentals, the competent use of skills, and command over subject matter—not mere passing grades. Mastery of what is taught must be America's standard of educational excellence, and schools need to offer the comprehensive curriculum and provide the time and resources that can make this mastery an achievable goal.

Principle Two:
Students must be active participants in learning. Students must become questioners and explorers, not just passive recipients of information. That active involvement demands learning environments free from disruptive behavior—and learning activities designed to encourage student initiative.

Principle Three:
Full learning opportunity must be available for all students. All students must be provided learning opportunities that enable them to fully realize their individual potential, regardless of their economic, social, physical or psychological condition.

Principle Four:
Learning should occur throughout life. Appropriate opportunities for learning must be available in all school districts for all age groups.

Principle Five:
Authority must be vested in the local faculty. Key decisions about teaching and learning should be made by those closest to students and the community, rather than by large bureaucracies whose assembly line approach diminishes expectations of students and teachers.

Principle Six:
School staff must be professionally compensated. Teacher salaries must become commensurate with those in comparable professions if the nation is to attract and retain the best teachers.

Principle Seven:
There must be high standards for teacher preparation and practice. Professional competence must be rooted in intellectually stimulating and demanding teacher preparation programs, rigorous personnel evaluation procedures, and meaningful professional and staff development programs.

Principle Eight:
School/community resources must be coordinated to benefit students. Problems that affect students' ability to learn must be resolved by school/community collaboration and coordination.

Principle Nine:
Adequate financial support for education is essential. Excellence in education depends on the combined resources of federal, state and local governments.

1986

Sharon Christa McAuliffe
September 2,1948-January 28,1986
''I touch the future. I teach.''

When the space shuttle Challenger exploded on January 28, 1986, taking the lives of the seven crew members including Christa McAuliffe, NEA member and social studies teacher from Concord, New Hampshire, words of sorrow and regret somehow weren't enough to express the feelings of the nation's devastated teachers and students.

NEA decided that words, no matter how eloquent, didn't really represent the vibrant, caring educator, wife and mother who had so courageously become the first private citizen—and teacher—in space. Therefore, the Association created a living memorial, the Christa McAuliffe Education Fund. This fund, administered by the National Foundation for the Improvement of Education (NFIE), will provide grants to individual teachers and groups of teachers to experiment with imaginative teaching approaches or to study for the purpose of professional growth.

Speaking to the 1986 Representative Assembly, Steven McAuliffe, Christa's husband, reminded NEA members everywhere of Christa's deep commitment to improving the quality of education: ''If you sit on the sidelines, reflect back on Christa as hero or glorious representative or canonized saint, rather than putting your entire energies into accomplishing for her what she wanted to do, then I think her efforts will have been in vain. . . .I hope you will use Christa's efforts and her spirit to get involved in the political arena effectively. To recruit and elect education candidates. To unseat those who support education with their words but not with their appropriations.''

Christa McAuliffe-
. . .teacher, mother, astronaut, Association member.

Outrage at the continuing violence and injustice in South Africa promoted the World Confederation of Organizations of the Teaching Profession (WCOTP) to adopt a resolution on apartheid and sanctions that had been submitted to the Assembly by the NEA delegation. Citing atrocities against children, the resolution stated, in part: "During the 1985 state of emergency nearly one-third of those detained by the South African government were children under the age of 16. Two thousand students. . .were detained and many held for months before their release. At least 201 children were killed by security forces; 11-year-olds were charged with political offenses and denied bail. Torture in detention is rampant; at a minimum, 15 persons died in police custody or immediately after release. Most of these were younger than 25, including a thirteen-year-old boy. . . ." The resolution calls for an end to all trade and commerce until the South African government ends the measures now employed and negotiates with "leaders selected by the majority peoples toward the end of establishing a multiracial, democratic government and a free and just society in South Africa."

WCOTP, founded in 1952 with NEA's assistance, represents 7 million teachers in 85 nations. The organization works to improve both the quality of education and to defend teachers' individual and collective rights.

NFIE Launches Operation Rescue. The National Foundation for the Improvement of Education (NFIE), NEA's educational and charitable tax-exempt institution created to improve education, has launched a major program with NEA to help solve the school dropout problems rampant throughout the United States.

Each year, about 700,000 students drop out—and those who do are often unemployed for long periods of time; still others are trapped in low-paying, dead-end jobs. Minority student dropouts are a special problem; as many as 50 percent of all Hispanic students drop out; 44 percent of all blacks do so; and up to 85 percent of all American Indian students leave school without graduating. NEA is committed to a nationwide campaign—"Operation Rescue"—to attempt to reduce these frightening statistics, in half if possible, by 1990. Through NFIE, $700,000 grants are available to local Associations for beginning or strengthening locally designed dropout prevention programs.

In the years since its creation in 1969, NFIE has administered more than 40 projects and generated more than $7 million in grants and contracts from foundations, government agencies, corporations and individuals. Many of the projects NFIE funds take a practical approach to problem solving in the classroom by teachers and students. Still others contribute to classroom creativity. In all, NFIE projects today are designed to help educators and their students find better ways to learn and grow.

Teacher testing in two states—Arkansas and Texas—served as a source of anger and declining morale when employed teachers were forced by action of the states' governors and legislators to take and pass what amounted to simple literacy tests to retain their teaching certificates.

Problems began in Arkansas in 1985 when Governor Clinton made teacher testing the cornerstone of a limited education reform program for the state. A recent court ruling mandated an equalization program for Arkansas schools, meaning that the bill for education would go higher. The teacher testing program was offered as "proof" that education quality in the state would improve as the state sales tax was increased as the means for more money for schools. Teachers, enraged that doubts would be cast on their basic competency, regardless of how many years of proven

successful teaching they'd completed, reacted with protests and efforts to prevent the enactment of the enabling legislation. The law passed on a tide of public sentiment for "education reform," and the first wave of testing showed the overwhelming majority of Arkansas educators to have passed. All that had been lost was $3 million in state revenues that could have been used to help schools—and the dignity of Arkansas educators.

In Texas, 99.1% of all educators successfully passed the TECAT—the Texas Examination for Current Administrators and Teachers—and almost the same percentage of the state's educators resented both the challenge to their competence and education and the waste of state revenues (more than $7 million) that TECAT represented.

The frenzy to link "education reform" with forced basic literacy testing of employed educators has not spread to other states. While there is ample support for requiring those entering the profession to pass qualifying exams, almost no one condones the notion of disregarding what can be decades of successful teaching to administer literacy exams to practicing educators.

The 1980's, like each decade before, has brought new issues of educational and social concern for Association members.

Pay equity, record numbers of dropouts, the health hazard of asbestos in school buildings, sexual harrassment, standardized personnel practices—all these have served to focus educator energies throughout the nation, and in all areas of Association membership.

The issue of **pay equity** has emerged as an especially critical concern to the Association's educational support members. In Maine, the Association's classified Higher Education unit was one of the first to tackle the problem. And today, support staff members in the Classified Employees Association of the San Diego Unified School District in California and the Classified School Employees Association of Clark County (Las Vegas) Nevada are working together in a major program to develop an appropriate job reclassification system based on pay equity. The project is

designed to study pay equity issues fully, and to develop a model program that local Associations throughout the nation can use in the years ahead.

The CSEA of Clark County, Nevada has also been successful recently in revising school district policy in regard to **sexual harassment.** Problems in this area drew CSEA's attention when harassment caused a CSEA member to resign from the district in 1985. CSEA has been able to persuade the woman to return to the district in a different position, and charges have been filed against the school administrator involved. CSEA then explored the problem in depth and found that there were more, similar incidents in evidence. CSEA worked with school district administration and has been successful in the adoption of reasonably clear and specific language detailing prohibited behaviors.

*   *   *

Recent statistics show that on in four students in eighth grade today will leave school without graduating. In today's competitive work environment, the nation's **dropout** victims are unlikely to be able to find rewarding employment. NEA decided to address the problem where it happens—at the local level—by a program that awards grants to local Associations beginning or strengthening locally designed dropout prevention programs. This program, begun in 1986 by decision of the Representative Assembly, is managed through NEA's National Foundation for the Improvement of Education (NFIE).

*   *   *

Cancer-causing **asbestos** continues to be a problem in many school districts throughout the nation. NEA's 1985 survey of school districts to assess the dimensions of the problem in school buildings revealed that nearly 75% of districts had friable (crumbling) asbestos. Other surveys conducted by the American Association of School Administrators (AASA) and the U.S. Government Accounting Office reveal similar findings. Costs of correcting the problem are high, averaging well over $100,000 per district; more than $86 million has already been spent nationwide on correction. Maintenance and custodial workers are in the greatest danger of coming into direct contact with asbestos because of the likelihood that their work will take them into parts of school buildings where asbestos was most frequently used. NEA has succeeded in lobbying effectively for federal monies for assistance in school district cleanup efforts. However, the more than $100 million from federal sources thus far isn't enough to enable all the nation's districts to do all that is necessary. Association members everywhere must continue to be vigilant in ensuring that this potential killer ceases to present a threat to students and school employees throughout the nation.

CONCLUSION

In 1987, NEA, with more than 1.8 million members, is the largest employee organization in the United States. One hundred and thirty years ago there were only 43 members. It has been an interesting journey.

The story of the National Education Association is primarily a story of people—highly individualistic, opinionated, creative and dedicated people—who had sufficient courage and faith to work energetically to realize a dream for our profession, and a dream of quality education for every child in the United States.

Today's NEA remains an organization dedicated to the same basic goals that the 43 founders expressed in 1857: the advancement of the profession and the improvement of public education.

Today's NEA works to represent its membership with all the skill and energy a dedicated leadership and staff can muster. We know that our strength lies in cooperation and mutual understanding.

We take careful and considered note of the world around us, and acknowledge that without efforts to create a world at peace, in which justice prevails and the dignity of human life is paramount, there cannot be an environment in which all may learn and grow.

We are a grassroots organization of individuals who have come together in free choice—and that is our great strength. The advancement of member rights is central to all that we do; it is our primary responsibility and welcomed obligation.

We are pledged to fight all those who would deny opportunities to all, and we shall do so, year after year, until the voices of bigotry and hate are stilled.

The generations that came before us and worked in the profession struggled with the central issues of their day, and built a system of free public education for all that has no rival anywhere in the world. The teachers built that system, often at great personal sacrifice. Today's school employees have the same challenge—to preserve what we have that is good in our schools, and, above all, to continue to secure the educational improvements that our changing democracy demands.

The National Education Association—proud, diverse, growing stronger all the time—is equal to that challenge.

IMPORTANT DATES IN NEA HISTORY

1857
August 26th—the National Teachers Association is founded in Philadelphia, Pennsylvania.

1861
In Springfield, Ohio, a group of black educators forms the Ohio Colored Teachers' Association—the first recorded organization of black teachers.

1862
The Land Grant Act (Morrill Act) passes; this paved the way for the creation of state university systems. NTA lobbied for passage of this legislation.

1866
Women are admitted to full membership in the Association.

1867
A U.S. Department of Education is created, representing NTA's first major legislative victory. However, the new Department is not given Cabinet status.

1868
NTA holds its first convention in the South, in Nashville.

1870
NTA becomes the National Education Association by assimilating three small groups.

1884
This year's convention draws more than 5,000 educators, launching a significant membership and financial breakthrough for the young Association.

1887
NEA passes a resolution insisting on retirement plans for teachers in all states.

1894
NEA's "Committee of Ten" recommends the structure for American public high schools; the recommendations receive widespread acceptance.

1898
NEA employs its first full-time executive secretary, Irwin Shepard.

1903
The NEA National Committee on Salaries, Tenure and Pensions is created to address improvements in these areas for teachers.

1904
Saline County, Illinois teachers organize public support for livable salaries and working conditions, prevailing over the school board.

The National Colored Teachers Association is created by J.R.E. Lee, Dean of the Academic Department of Tuskegee Institute. (The Association was renamed the National Association of Teachers in Colored Schools in 1907.)

Booker T. Washington addresses the NEA Convention in St. Louis, Missouri.

1905
The first NEA teacher salary study is published. The study included recommendations on ways to adequately fund public schools.

1906
NEA is incorporated by an Act of Congress as the National Education Association of the United States.

1907
NEA is fifty years old, and has 5,044 members.

1909
The first State tenure law for teachers is enacted in New Jersey.

1910
Ella Flagg Young becomes the first woman President of NEA.

1911
NEA endorses women's suffrage.

1913
The NEA Department of Classroom Teachers is founded.

The *NEA Bulletin* begins publication—the NEA's first professional journal.

1917
NEA moves permanently to Washington, D.C.

James W. Crabtree becomes the NEA executive secretary.

1918
Memphis teachers strike and win higher salaries.

NEA issues the "Cardinal Principles of Education."

1919
NEA Commission on the Emergency in Education issues "Teacher Salaries and Salary Schedules in the United States," and uses the document to rally public support for schools. This marked the Association's renewed push for federal funds for public education.

New Jersey becomes the first state to have a statewide teacher retirement system.

1920
NEA becomes governed by a Representative Assembly of elected delegates, rather than continuing to have policy making done by whomever showed up at each year's Convention.

1921
The *NEA Journal*, a professional magazine, begins publication.

The President of the United States is petitioned by NEA and the heads of many other national organizations to create a Cabinet-level "Department of Education."

American Education Week is created by NEA, the American Legion and the U.S. Office of Education.

1922
NEA Research is established.

1923
The World Federation of Education Associations is founded, with NEA's assistance and support.

Mary McLeod Bethune becomes the first woman president of the National Association of Teachers in Colored Schools.

1924
"The Fundamental Principles of a Teachers' Retirement System" is issued by NEA; this publication helps state Associations secure retirement programs for teachers.

1926
The first Joint Committee of NEA and the National Association of Teachers in Colored Schools (NATCS) is created, to study the problems of the education of blacks in general, and in particular to find ways to have black secondary schools accredited, thereby enabling black graduates to gain admittance to the nation's institutions of higher education.

1928
The NEA-NATCS Joint Committee becomes permanent. Both groups agree that representatives of each organization will attend the respective conventions of the other body, that prominent black educators will address the conventions of NEA and that the problems of the inadequate quality of education available to blacks, especially in the South, would be addressed.

1929
NEA Code of Ethics is adopted.

1930
The second NEA Commission on the Emergency in Education is created to assist schools and teachers during the Depression.

1935
The "Little Red Rider" is attached to a D.C. school appropriations bill, forcing teachers to sign loyalty oaths; NEA works for repeal, and is successful in 1937.

1937
The National Association of Teachers in Colored Schools becomes the American Teachers Association (ATA).

1941
NEA President Donald DuShane creates the National Committee for the Defense of Democracy to fund the legal defense of teachers whose rights are violated. It is known today as the Kate Frank/DuShane Fund.

The Lanham Act passes Congress, creating impact aid (federal monies for school districts in which substantial numbers of federal workers live); NEA lobbied for passage.

1942
NEA succeeds in securing exemptions for teachers under the Hatch Act.

1943
NEA Representative Assembly votes to refuse to meet in any city denying equal accommodations to all, regardless of race.

NEA begins publication of a regular newsletter for Association leaders.

The Kate Frank case begins in Muskogee, Oklahoma. Kate Frank and several other teachers are dismissed for supporting candidates for the school board. Kate Frank decides to fight her discharge, and the Association agrees to provide financial help.

1944

NEA's Division of Legislative and Federal Relations is created.

NEA lobbying helps to secure passage of the G.I. Bill.

1945

The Kate Frank case is won, and the remaining monies are used to form the Du-Shane Fund.

1946

Norwalk, Connecticut teachers strike to secure a written contract with the school board.

NEA TEPS (Teacher Education and Professional Standards) Commission is created.

1947

NEA affiliates 18 black education Associations in Southern and border states and the District of Columbia, because laws there prohibited black teachers from joining white organizations.

1952

The World Confederation of Organizations of the Teaching Profession is founded, with NEA assistance.

1953

William G. Carr becomes NEA executive secretary.

NEA becomes the first national organization to conduct major salary research in higher education.

Construction begins on NEA's Washington Headquarters.

1954

The United States Supreme Court rules, in *Brown v. Board of Education*, that public schools must desegregate.

NCATE, the National Council for Accreditation of Teacher Education, is created.

1957

NEA is 100 years old. United States President Dwight D. Eisenhower assists in the celebration by cutting the Association birthday cake at the annual convention held in Philadelphia, where the Association was born in 1857.

1958

NEA starts "salary schools," hires salary consultants to assist affiliates in negotiations.

1959

Wisconsin becomes the first state to enact a collective bargaining law for public employees.

1961

NEA creates the Professional Rights & Responsibilities Commission for the defense of teacher rights.

1962

NEA passes a strong resolution urging school boards to negotiate in good faith with teacher Associations.

The *NEA REPORTER,* the Association monthly tabloid newspaper (named NEA TODAY now), begins publication.

1963

NEA published "Guidelines for Professional Negotiations;" within a year, more than 750,000 copies are in use.

1964

The NEA Representative Assembly passes Resolution 12, requiring racially separated state affiliates to merge.

1965

The Elementary & Secondary School Act (ESEA), providing schools with the nation's first major infusion of federal financial aid, is signed into law by President Lyndon Johnson. NEA helped draft the legislation.

NEA helps teachers in a difficult voter registration drive in Selma, Alabama.

1966

The American Teachers Association (ATA) and NEA merge.

1967

NEA has one million members.

Dr. Sam Lambert becomes NEA executive secretary.

The NEA Board of Directors votes to support affiliates on strike.

NEA staff secures the right to bargain with NEA.

1968

Elizabeth Duncan Koontz becomes the first black president of NEA.

The U.S. Supreme Court ruling in *Maryland v. Wirtz* encourages public employee organizations like NEA to mount a drive to secure a federal collective bargaining law for public employees.

The Bilingual Education Act passes after three years of NEA lobbying efforts.

The National Foundation for the Improvement of Education (NFIE) is created by NEA.

1969
NEA enters the arena of national politics by publicly opposing the nomination of Clement F. Haynesworth for the Supreme Court because of his negative record on civil rights. The nomination of Harrold Carswell in early 1970 was opposed by NEA for the same reason.

NEA and other national organizations with an interest in public education create the Coalition for Full Funding, to lobby together for increases in federal funds for schools.

1970
Hawaii and Pennsylvania enact public employee collective bargaining laws that give public workers the legal right to strike.

NEA's UniServ staffing program is begun nationwide.

NEA mounts major task forces in Mississippi and Louisiana to help affiliates there cope with problems arising from the school desegregation process.

Minority caucuses form within NEA.

1971
NEA's Instruction & Professional Development Unit is created.

Con-Con, the Association's Constitutional Convention, begins its work.

1972
NEA, AFSCME and other public employee groups form the Coalition of American Public Employees (CAPE), to work cooperatively for the passage of a federal collective bargaining law for public workers.

NEA-PAC endorses its first federal candidates for public office.

Allan West becomes NEA interim executive secretary.

The NEA Teacher Rights unit is created.

The NEA Representative Assembly votes formal support for passage of the Equal Rights Amendment.

NEA wins the *Sinderman/Roth* cases at the U.S. Supreme Court level; important rights for higher education faculty are protected.

1973
Terry Herndon becomes the executive secretary of NEA.

NEA's new Constitution is approved by the Representative Assembly.

1974
NEA sets its procedure for the endorsement of a candidate for the position of President of the United States.

Merger talks with AFT, AFL-CIO end.

NEA wins a major case in the U.S. Supreme Court, striking down mandatory maternity leave for pregnant teachers.

Congress approves funding for the NEA-backed teacher centers.

1975
Public law 94-142, Education for All Handicapped Children, is enacted into law. NEA helped secure passage.

James Harris becomes NEA's second black president.

The NEA Representative Assembly votes to hold no meetings in states that fail to ratify the Equal Rights Amendment.

1976
All states are now fully unified with NEA.

NEA, for the first time in Association history, endorses candidates for President and Vice-President of the United States—Jimmy Carter and Walter Mondale.

1977
The NEA Representative Assembly votes not to endorse any candidate for federal office who opposes ERA.

1979
A Cabinet-level Department of Education becomes law, and NEA's dream of more than 100 years is realized.

All state Associations now have functional affirmative action plans.

1980

Educational Support Personnel are voted full membership rights in NEA by the Representative Assembly.

NEA sends 464 members as delegates or alternates to the Democratic National Convention—more than any other organization or union. Twenty-two members attend the Republican Convention.

1981

The NEA Representative Assembly raises more than $50,000 to support efforts to pass ERA.

1982

NEA issues a major *Action Plan* for the reform of teacher education. The *Plan* becomes a blueprint for state action.

The NEA-Retired program is instituted.

The Congress of Faculty Associations—NEA's affiliate—defeats AFT in higher education's largest and most significant bargaining election, covering 19,000 faculty members in California.

1983

Martin Luther King, Jr.'s birthday becomes a federal holiday; NEA had lobbied for passage for many years.

Mary Hatwood Futrell is elected NEA president; she is the Association's third black president.

Don Cameron becomes executive director of NEA.

The Representative Assembly creates the Blue-Ribbon Task Force on Educational Excellence to present NEA's position on educational reform.

1984

The thirtieth anniversary of *Brown v. Board of Education* is commemorated by NEA with a report on three cities where desegregation has been successful, and where the efforts of local affiliates helped to make the difference.

The Blue Ribbon Task Force Report is approved by the Representative Assembly and issued to educators and the general public as *An Open Letter to America on Schools, Students and Tomorrow*. The document proposed revolutionary changes needed to improve American public education.

The School Hazard Abatement Act passes Congress, authorizing funds to help eliminate dangerous asbestos from the public schools; NEA lobbied for passage.

NEA holds the first satellite telecast to affiliates via EdNet, the nation's first satellite TV network operated by an education or labor organization.

1985

The Association embraces the *Nine Principles of Education* to guide the profession in progress toward meaningful education reform recommended in *An Open Letter to America*.

NEA lobbies for the Civil Rights Restoration Act, designed to restrengthen prohibitions against sex discrimination in any institution receiving federal monies.

NEA becomes the nation's largest employee organization.

1986

NEA membership surpasses 1.8 million.

Christa McAuliffe, NEA member and social studies teacher who was to be the nation's first teacher in space, dies with the other astronauts on the shuttle *Challenger*. NEA creates a living memorial, the Christa McAuliffe Education Fund, to provide grants to individual teachers and groups of teachers to experiment with imaginative teaching approaches or to study for the purposes of professional growth.

NEA launches a nationwide dropout prevention program. The campaign, called Operation Rescue, is run by the National Foundation for the Improvement of Education and awards grants to local Associations for beginning or strengthening locally designed dropout prevention programs.